KIM DIEHL

Simple Whatnots II

A Second Helping of Satisfyingly Scrappy Quilts

Martingale®
Create with Confidence

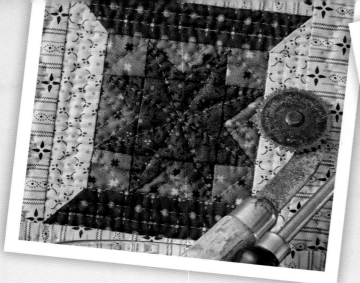

Simple Whatnots II:
A Second Helping of Satisfyingly Scrappy Quilts
© 2021 by Kim Diehl

Martingale®
18939 120th Ave. NE, Ste. 101
Bothell, WA 98011-9511 USA
ShopMartingale.com

Printed in Hong Kong
26 25 24 23 22 21   8 7 6 5 4 3 2 1

Library of Congress Cataloging-in-Publication Data is available upon request.

ISBN: 978-1-68356-124-8

MISSION STATEMENT

We empower makers who use fabric and yarn to make life more enjoyable.

CREDITS

**PUBLISHER AND
CHIEF VISIONARY OFFICER**
Jennifer Erbe Keltner

CONTENT DIRECTOR
Karen Costello Soltys

DESIGN MANAGER
Adrienne Smitke

TECHNICAL EDITOR
Laurie Baker

PRODUCTION MANAGER
Regina Girard

COPY EDITOR
Melissa Bryan

LOCATION PHOTOGRAPHER
Adam Albright

ILLUSTRATOR
Sandy Loi

STUDIO PHOTOGRAPHER
Brent Kane

Contents

Introduction 5

Simple Whatnots II Projects

Tongue and Groove 7

Spooling Around 13

Cloud Nine 19

Cracker Crumbs 27

Cotton Blossoms 33

Skip to My Lou 41

Double Dutch Stars 47

Chicken Scratch Patch 51

Hickory Dickory 57

Esther's Garden Box 63

Fair and Square 69

Old Glory 75

Prairie Sky 83

Matchsticks 89

Idaho Lily 95

Henpecked 103

Linen Drawer 109

Tussie-Mussie 113

Kim's Quiltmaking Basics 119

About the Author 128

Introduction

As a little girl, when Christmas, special holidays, and birthdays rolled around, I always heard my mama tell me that good things come in small packages. And she was so right! I learned at an early age that the littlest gifts were often the best, and the same holds true with small quilts . . . they're like Christmas and your birthday all wrapped up into one sweet little package.

I love blending and sprinkling quilts both small and large generously throughout my home to create an air of warmth and welcome. Large quilts are what I consider to be the building blocks that help anchor the look and feel of each room, but it's the addition of thoughtfully placed little quilts that really ramps up the atmosphere, creates small islands of color, and lends a bit of sparkle. Through the years I've learned that nearly any big quilt can be made small, and a tiny bit of magic happens when you reduce a design from grand in scale to petite in size—the resulting minis are like little bits of pixie dust straight from the sewing room!

This collection of little quilts features 12 favorites from my Simple Whatnots Club with Henry Glass Fabrics and, to sweeten the deal, I've slipped six fresh new designs into the lineup for a total of 18 projects just begging to be stitched! You'll find that this batch of quilts includes a variety of sizes, shapes, and skill levels to suit your every mood. One of the things I love most about this collection is that many of the projects are scrappy, making them ideal stash busters.

To help you achieve fantastic results as you stitch and use your small quilts, you'll find little hints and helps in the form of "Extra Snippets" scattered throughout this book. Some of these tidbits of information are things that helped me be successful as I worked through the project steps, and others offer a variety of suggestions and ideas for living with and making the most of your handiwork.

Ultimately, my best advice is to remember that quiltmaking is a journey. Sometimes there are small bumps in the road—just skip on past them and don't let them slow you down. As we tackle each new project, our skills naturally improve, so don't be overly hard on yourself if you miss the tip of a star point or stitch an intersection that doesn't quite intersect. Mistakes are simply learning opportunities in disguise, and when you stitch each new block and quilt to the best of your abilities, you'll see your skills flourish and grow!

Happy small stitching,

~ Kim

Tongue and Groove

If you've been looking for that perfect first project to get your appliqué groove on, look no more! The tongue shapes in this little quilt are super easy to master even if you've never sewn a stitch of appliqué, and the scrappy mix of prints sparkles like jewels.

Materials

Yardage is based on a 42" usable width of fabric after prewashing and removing selvages.

- 1 fat eighth (9" × 21") of black print A for blocks
- 1 fat eighth of black print B for blocks
- 36 charm squares (5" × 5") of assorted prints *or* approximately ⅞ yard of assorted print scraps for blocks and border
- 1 fat quarter (18" × 21") of black print C for border
- 1 fat quarter of complementary print for binding
- ⅝ yard of fabric for backing
- 21" × 21" square of batting
- Supplies for your favorite appliqué method

Cutting

Cut all pieces across the width of the fabric in the order given unless otherwise noted. Step-by-step instructions for my invisible machine-appliqué method begin on page 121, or you can substitute your own favorite method. The large and small tongue appliqué patterns are provided on page 11.

From black print A, cut:
3 strips, 2½" × 21"; crosscut into 18 squares, 2½" × 2½"

From black print B, cut:
3 strips, 2½" × 21"; crosscut into 18 squares, 2½" × 2½"

From *each* of 28 charm squares, cut:
1 square, 2½" × 2½" (combined total of 28)
1 large tongue appliqué (combined total of 28)
1 small tongue appliqué (combined total of 28)

From *each* of the remaining 8 charm squares, cut:
1 large tongue appliqué (grand total of 36, with previously cut appliqués)
1 small tongue appliqué (grand total of 36, with previously cut appliqués)

From black print C, cut:
6 strips, 1¾" × 21"; crosscut into 56 squares, 1¾" × 1¾"

From the binding print, cut:
4 strips, 2½" × 21" (for my chubby-binding method provided on page 127, reduce the strip width to 2")

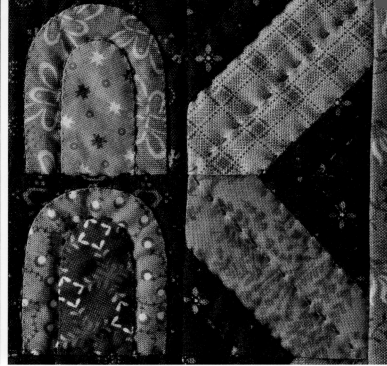

Appliquéing the Blocks

1. Fold each black A and B 2½" square in half, right sides together, and use a hot, dry iron to lightly press a center vertical crease.

2. Fold each large and small tongue appliqué in half vertically, right sides together, and finger-press a crease.

3. Choosing the prints randomly, select a large and small tongue appliqué. Position the large appliqué onto a prepared black A square, with the bottom raw edges flush and the vertical creases aligned to perfectly center the appliqué from side to side. Pin or baste the appliqué in place. Use your favorite method to stitch the appliqué to the black square. In the same manner, add and stitch the small appliqué. Repeat to appliqué 18 black A blocks. Using the black B squares, repeat to appliqué a total of 18 black B blocks. Each block should measure 2½" square, including the seam allowances.

Center crease   Center crease

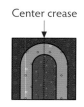

Make 18 A blocks,   Make 18 B blocks,
2½" × 2½".   2½" × 2½".

Piecing the Quilt Center

Sew all pieces with right sides together using a ¼" seam allowance. Press the seam allowances as indicated by the arrows or otherwise specified.

1. Lay out three appliquéd black A squares and three appliquéd black B squares in alternating positions. Join the squares. Press. Repeat to piece a total of three #1 rows measuring 2½" × 12½", including the seam allowances.

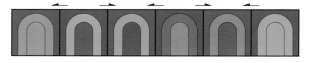

Make 3 of row #1,
2½" × 12½".

2. Repeat step 1, reversing the positions of the black A and B squares, to piece a total of three #2 rows measuring 2½" × 12½", including the seam allowances.

Make 3 of row #2,
2½" × 12½".

3. Lay out the #1 and #2 rows in alternating positions to form the quilt center. Join the rows. Press. The pieced quilt center should measure 12½" square, including the seam allowances.

Quilt assembly

PIECING AND ADDING THE BORDER

1. Use a pencil and an acrylic ruler to draw a diagonal sewing line from corner to corner on the wrong side of each black C 1¾" square. Layer a prepared black C square onto one corner of a print 2½" square as shown. Stitch the pair together along the drawn line. Fold the resulting inner black triangle open, aligning the corner with the corner of the bottommost square. Press. Trim away the layers beneath the top triangle, leaving a ¼" seam allowance. In the same manner, add a black C triangle to the opposite corner of the square. Repeat to piece a total of 28 border blocks measuring 2½" square, including the seam allowances.

Make 28 border blocks,
2½" × 2½".

Savor Your Quilt Display

Wine racks can provide a perfect and unexpected way to showcase your small quilts, and best of all, there are tons of styles and sizes available to suit your decorating needs. Simply choose a variety of little quilts that "play nicely" and complement each other, and then fold, roll, and slide them into the bottle openings. You'll discover there's no need to display these little works of art completely open, because when grouped together in this way, they make a huge impact!

FINISHED QUILT SIZE: 16½" × 16½" • **FINISHED BLOCK SIZE: 2" × 2"**

Designed, appliquéd, pieced, and hand quilted by Kim Diehl.

2. Lay out six border blocks end to end in a zigzag pattern. Join the blocks. Press. Repeat to piece a total of four zigzag border strips measuring 2½" × 12½", including the seam allowances. Reserve the remaining four border blocks.

Make 4 border strips,
2½" × 12½".

3. Referring to the quilt assembly diagram, join a zigzag border strip to the right and left sides of the quilt center. Press. Join a reserved border block to each end of the remaining two zigzag border strips. Press. Join these strips to the top and bottom edges of the quilt center. Press.

Adding the border

COMPLETING THE QUILT

Layer and baste the quilt top, batting, and backing. Quilt the layers. The featured quilt was hand quilted in the big-stitch method with the appliqués outlined to emphasize their shapes, and all quilt-center blocks were stitched in the ditch (along the seam lines). The zigzag border was stitched in the ditch, with echoed V-shaped lines stitched in the black portions of the blocks, and the assorted print portions stitched from corner to corner through the center. Join the binding strips to make one length and use it to bind the quilt.

Patterns do not include seam allowances.

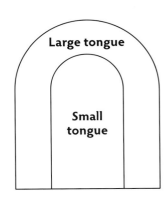

Large tongue

Small tongue

Spooling Around

There's something so completely satisfying about merging favorite patchwork motifs into one new and unique block. This sweet and petite quilt is quick to piece, super approachable if you'd like to dabble in a little hand quilting, and easy to nestle into the smallest of spaces!

MATERIALS

Yardage is based on a 42" usable width of fabric after prewashing and removing selvages.

- 8 charm squares (5" × 5") of assorted prints for block stars and star backgrounds
- Scraps at least 3" × 5½" *each* of 4 assorted brown prints for spools
- 1 fat eighth (9" × 21") of cream print A for blocks
- 1 fat eighth of cream print B for sashing and inner border
- 1 fat eighth of medium blue print for middle border
- 1 fat eighth of chestnut print for sashing square and outer border
- 1 fat quarter (18" × 21") of dark brown print for binding
- ⅝ yard of fabric for backing
- 20" × 20" square of batting

CUTTING

Cut all pieces across the width of the fabric in the order given, unless otherwise noted. Separate the assorted print charm squares into 4 prints for the stars and 4 prints for the star backgrounds.

From *each* of the 4 charm squares chosen for the stars, cut:

1 square, 2" × 2" (combined total of 4)
8 squares, 1¼" × 1¼" (combined total of 32)
Keep the pieces organized by print into star sets.

From *each* of the 4 charm squares chosen for the star backgrounds, cut:

3 strips, 1¼" × 5"; crosscut into:
    4 rectangles, 1¼" × 2" (combined total of 16)
    4 squares, 1¼" × 1¼" (combined total of 16)
Keep the pieces organized by print into star background sets.

From *each* of the 4 assorted brown prints, cut:

2 rectangles, 1¼" × 5" (combined total of 8)

From cream print A, cut:

3 strips, 1¼" × 21"; crosscut into:
    16 squares, 1¼" × 1¼"
    8 rectangles, 1¼" × 3½"

From cream print B, cut:

4 strips, 1¼" × 21"; crosscut into:
    2 rectangles, 1¼" × 11¾"
    2 rectangles, 1¼" × 10¼"
    4 rectangles, 1¼" × 5"

From the medium blue print, cut:

4 strips, 1" × 21"; crosscut into:
    2 rectangles, 1" × 11¾"
    2 rectangles, 1" × 12¾"

From the chestnut print, cut:

4 strips, 1¾" × 21"; crosscut into:
    2 rectangles, 1¾" × 12¾"
    2 rectangles, 1¾" × 15¼"
1 square, 1¼" × 1¼"

From the dark brown print, cut:

4 binding strips, 2½" × 21" (for my chubby-binding method provided on page 127, reduce the strip width to 2")

square in three horizontal rows. Join the pieces in each row. Press. Join the rows. Press. The pieced star unit should measure 3½" square, including the seam allowances.

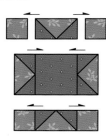

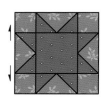

Star unit,
3½" × 3½".

PIECING THE SPOOL BLOCKS

Sew all pieces with right sides together using a ¼" seam allowance. Press the seam allowances as indicated by the arrows or otherwise specified.

1. Select one set of star print patchwork pieces, one set of complementary star background print pieces, two brown 1¼" × 5" rectangles cut from a single print, two cream A 1¼" × 3½" rectangles, and four cream A 1¼" squares. Use a pencil and an acrylic ruler to draw a diagonal sewing line from corner to corner on the wrong side of each of the eight star-print 1¼" squares and the four cream 1¼" squares. Set the prepared cream squares aside for later use.

2. Layer a prepared 1¼" star square onto one end of a star background 1¼" × 2" rectangle. Stitch the pair together along the drawn line. Fold the resulting inner triangle open, aligning the corner with the corner of the rectangle. Press. Trim away the layers beneath the top triangle, leaving a ¼" seam allowance. In the same manner, use a second prepared 1¼" star square to add a mirror-image triangle to the remaining end of the rectangle. Repeat to piece a total of four star-point units measuring 1¼" × 2", including the seam allowances.

Make 4 star-point units,
1¼" × 2".

3. Lay out the four star-point units, the four star background 1¼" squares, and one star print 2" center

4. Using the reserved prepared cream A 1¼" squares and the two brown 1¼" × 5" rectangles, refer to step 2 to stitch a triangle and a mirror-image triangle to the rectangle ends as shown. The two pieced brown rectangles should measure 1¼" × 5", including the seam allowances.

Make 2 pieced rectangles,
1¼" × 5".

5. Lay out the two pieced brown rectangles, the star unit from step 3, and the two cream A 1¼" × 3½" rectangles in three horizontal rows. Join the cream rectangles to the star unit. Press. Join the rows. Press. The pieced Spool block should measure 5" square, including the seam allowances.

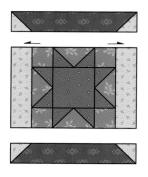

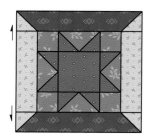

Spool block,
5" × 5"

6. Repeat steps 1–5 to piece a total of four Spool blocks.

FINISHED QUILT SIZE: 15¼" × 15¼" ✦ **FINISHED BLOCK SIZE:** 4½" × 4½"

Designed, pieced, and hand quilted by Kim Diehl.

PIECING THE QUILT CENTER

Lay out the four Spool blocks, the four cream B
1¼" × 5" rectangles, and the chestnut 1¼" square in
three horizontal rows. Join the pieces in each row.
Press. Join the rows. Press. The pieced quilt center
should measure 10¼" square, including the seam
allowances.

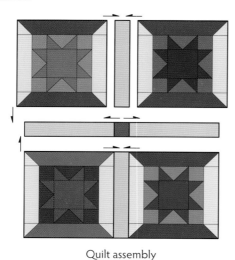

Quilt assembly

Quilt Bouquets

To easily display your little quilts, try
folding them with the bound edges
positioned in the center (I sometimes lay
a small hand towel on top of the folded
surface to add bulk and make them more
substantial), and then roll them up jelly
roll style. Arrange these rolled quilts into
a large basket or decorative container to
form a "bouquet," and then place them
on top of cabinets or cupboards to add an
extra pop of color to your room. Grouping
arranged baskets and adding additional
containers with little quilts spilled over
the brim makes a big impact in the room
and lets you take advantage of spaces that
might otherwise go unused.

ADDING THE BORDERS

Join a cream B 1¼" × 10¼" strip to the right and left sides of the quilt center. Press. Join the cream B 1¼" × 11¾" strips to the top and bottom edges of the quilt center to complete the inner border. Press. In the same manner, sew the shorter medium blue rectangles to the right and left sides of the quilt top and the longer medium blue rectangles to the top and bottom edges to complete the middle border. Finish by adding the short and long chestnut rectangles to the outer border. Press after the addition of each border rectangle.

COMPLETING THE QUILT

Layer and baste the quilt top, batting, and backing. Quilt the layers. The featured quilt was hand quilted with intersecting straight lines from point to point in the star centers, and the star shapes were outlined. Repeating straight lines were stitched onto the brown spool top and bottom pieces, and the spool shapes were echo quilted ¼" from the seam lines in the cream background areas. Serpentine lines were quilted through the center of the cream B sashing strips and inner border. The blue middle border was stitched in the ditch (along the seam lines), and a diagonal crosshatch was added to the outer chestnut border. Join the dark brown binding strips to make one length and use it to bind the quilt.

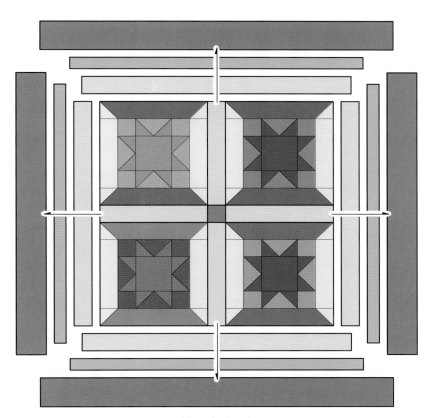

Adding the borders

Cloud Nine

Strategic piecing elevates the traditional yet humble Nine Patch blocks in this quilt, giving them the appearance of floating above the background. This sparkling patchwork mini may look complicated to stitch, but don't be fooled—the piecing is a snap, and fun!

MATERIALS

Yardage is based on a 42" usable width of fabric after prewashing and removing selvages.

- ⅝ yard of brown print for blocks, sashing squares, inner border, and binding
- ½ yard of cream print A for blocks and outer border
- ½ yard of cream print B for blocks and sashing strips
- 23 chubby sixteenths (9" × 10½") of assorted prints for blocks and outer border
- ⅞ yard of fabric for backing
- 29" × 29" square of batting

CUTTING

Cut all pieces across the width of the fabric in the order given unless otherwise noted.

From the brown print, cut:
6 strips, 1¼" × 42"; crosscut into:
    2 strips, 1¼" × 17"
    2 strips, 1¼" × 18½"
    128 squares, 1¼" × 1¼"
1 strip, 1" × 42"; crosscut into 9 squares, 1" × 1"
3 binding strips, 2½" × 42" (for my chubby-binding method provided on page 127, reduce the strip width to 2")

From cream print A, cut:
2 strips, 1¼" × 42"; crosscut into 64 squares, 1¼" × 1¼"
2 strips, 3½" × 42"; crosscut into 20 squares, 3½" × 3½"
1 strip, 2" × 42"; crosscut into 8 rectangles, 2" × 3½"

From cream print B, cut:
3 strips, 1¼" × 42"; crosscut into 64 rectangles, 1¼" × 1⅝"
4 strips, 1¼" × 42"; crosscut into 64 rectangles, 1¼" × 2⅜"
3 strips, 1" × 42"; crosscut into 24 rectangles, 1" × 4¼"

From *each* of the 23 assorted prints, cut:
3 squares, 1½" × 1½" (combined total of 69)
Reserve the remainder of the assorted prints.

From *each* of 16 of the reserved assorted prints, cut:
5 squares, 1¼" × 1¼" (combined total of 80)
Keep the squares organized by print. Reserve the remainder of the assorted prints.

From the remaining scraps of all assorted prints, cut a *combined total* of:
8 rectangles, 3½" × 6½"
16 squares, 2" × 2"
4 squares, 3½" × 3½"

PIECING THE BLOCKS

Sew all pieces with right sides together using a ¼" seam allowance. Press the seam allowances as indicated by the arrows or otherwise specified.

1. Select one set of five 1¼" squares cut from a single assorted print and four cream A 1¼" squares. Lay out the squares in three horizontal rows of three squares as shown. Join the squares in each row. Press. Join the rows. Press. Repeat to piece a total of 16 nine-patch units measuring 2¾" square, including the seam allowances.

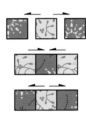

Make 16 units,
2¾" × 2¾".

2. Use a pencil and an acrylic ruler to draw a diagonal sewing line from corner to corner on the wrong side of each brown 1¼" square. Layer a prepared brown square onto one end of a cream B 1¼" × 1⅝" rectangle as shown. Stitch the pair together along the drawn line. Fold the resulting inner triangle open, aligning the corner with the corner of the cream rectangle. Trim away the excess layers beneath the top triangle, leaving a ¼" seam allowance. Repeat to piece a total of 32 short rectangle units and 32 mirror-image short rectangle units measuring 1¼" × 1⅝", including the seam allowances.

Make 32 of each short unit,
1¼" × 1⅝".

3. Using the remaining prepared brown 1¼" squares, and substituting the cream B 1¼" × 2⅜" rectangles for the smaller cream rectangles previously used, repeat step 2 to piece 32 long rectangle units and 32

mirror-image long rectangle units measuring 1¼" × 2⅜", including the seam allowances.

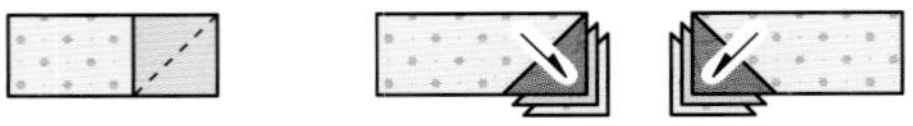

Make 32 of each long unit,
1¼" × 2⅜".

4. Join the brown ends of a pieced short rectangle unit and mirror-image unit from step 2. Press the seam allowances to one side, in whichever direction produces the best point. Repeat to piece a total of 32 short flying-geese units measuring 1¼" × 2¾", including the seam allowances.

Make 32 short flying-geese units,
1¼" × 2¾".

5. Repeat step 4, using the long rectangle units and mirror-image units from step 3, to piece 32 long flying-geese units measuring 1¼" × 4¼", including the seam allowances.

Make 32 long flying-geese units,
1¼" × 4¼".

6. Join a short flying-geese unit from step 4 to the right and left sides of each nine-patch unit from step 1. Press. Join a long flying-geese unit from step 5 to the top and bottom of each nine-patch unit. Press. Each patchwork block unit should measure 4¼" square, including the seam allowances.

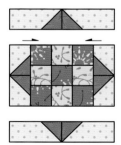 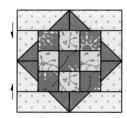

Make 16 patchwork block units,
4¼" × 4¼".

FINISHED QUILT SIZE: 24½" × 24½" ◆ **FINISHED BLOCK SIZE: 3¾" × 3¾"**

Designed and pieced by Kim Diehl. Machine quilted by Deborah Poole.

7. Draw a diagonal sewing line on the wrong side of each of the assorted print 1½" squares as previously instructed. Choosing the prints randomly, layer, stitch, press, and trim a triangle to each corner of a patchwork block unit as previously instructed. Repeat to piece a total of 16 blocks measuring 4¼" square, including the seam allowances. Please note that you'll have five unused assorted print squares; these have been included for added choices as you stitch the patchwork.

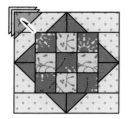 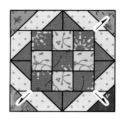

Make 16 blocks,
4¼" × 4¼".

PIECING THE QUILT CENTER

1. Referring to the quilt assembly diagram below, lay out four blocks and three cream B 1" × 4¼" rectangles in alternating positions. Join the pieces. Press. Repeat to piece a total of four block rows measuring 4¼" × 17", including the seam allowances.

2. Lay out four cream B 1¼" × 4¼" rectangles and three brown 1" squares in alternating positions. Join the pieces. Press. Repeat to piece a total of three sashing rows measuring 1" × 17", including the seam allowances.

3. Lay out the four block rows and three sashing rows in alternating positions. Join the rows. Press. The pieced quilt center should measure 17" square, including the seam allowances.

Quilt assembly

PIECING AND ADDING THE BORDERS

1. Referring to the quilt photo on page 21, join a brown 1¼" × 17" strip to the right and left sides of the quilt center. Press the seam allowances toward the brown strips. Join a brown 1¼" × 18½" strip to the top and bottom of the quilt center. Press the seam allowances toward the brown strips. The quilt top should measure 18½" square, including the seam allowances.

2. Draw a diagonal sewing line on the wrong side of 16 cream A 3½" squares and 16 assorted print 2" squares as previously instructed. Set the prepared assorted print squares aside for later use. Using a prepared cream square, layer, stitch, press, and trim

to make a triangle onto one end of a print 3½" × 6½" rectangle as previously instructed. Next, add a cream mirror-image triangle to the remaining end of the rectangle. Repeat to piece a total of eight flying-geese units measuring 3½" × 6½", including the seam allowances.

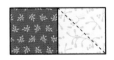   

Make 8 flying geese units,
3½" × 6½".

3. Using two prepared print 2" squares, layer, stitch, press, and trim to make triangles on two adjacent corners of a cream A 3½" square. Repeat to make a total of four pieced square units measuring 3½" square, including the seam allowances.

Make 4 pieced square units,
3½" × 3½".

4. Using one prepared print 2" square, layer, stitch, press, and trim to make a triangle on one end of a cream A 2" × 3½" rectangle. Repeat to make a total of four pieced rectangle units and four mirror-image rectangle units measuring 2" × 3½", including the seam allowances.

Make 4 of each rectangle unit,
2" × 3½".

5. Lay out one each of a pieced rectangle unit and a mirror-image rectangle unit, two pieced flying-geese units from step 2, and one pieced square unit from step 3 as shown. Join the pieces. Press. Repeat to piece a total of four outer-border rows measuring 3½" × 18½", including the seam allowances.

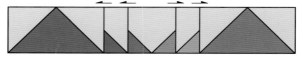

Make 4 border rows,
3½" × 18½".

6. Using the pictured quilt as a guide, join an outer-border row to the right and left sides of the quilt top. Press the seam allowances toward the inner border. Join a print 3½" square to each end of the remaining outer-border rows. Press the seam allowances toward the squares. Join these completed rows to the remaining sides of the quilt top.

COMPLETING THE QUILT

Layer and baste the quilt top, batting, and backing. Quilt the layers. The featured quilt was machine quilted with an overall swirling pattern (think cinnamon rolls!) in the quilt center, and the inner border was stitched in the ditch (along the seam lines). The small print triangles in the outer border were quilted with straight lines ¼" inside the sewn seams, and the large print triangles were stitched with repeating straight lines that intersect at the center to form diamonds. The cream border areas were stitched with repeating straight lines, and the corner squares were stitched with feathered Xs. Join the brown binding strips to make one length and use it to bind the quilt.

EXTRA SNIPPET

On a Roll

My new favorite repurposed find for organizing my binding is . . . a string holder! As I'm cutting fabrics for a new project, I prepare my binding so it's all ready to go when the top is finished. To make the string holder more functional for my purpose, I leave a couple layers of string around the center rod so I can anchor the binding end with a straight pin, then wind the binding onto the string holder. Anchoring with a pin lets me work my way up the holder with no "slippage," and I can store bindings for three or four mini-quilts at a time. When I'm ready to apply my binding, I carry the holder to my sewing area, unwinding the binding length as I use it. This keeps me beautifully organized with no tangled heaps of fabric to navigate. I found this rooster string holder in a local home-dec shop, but similar styles are also available through online retailers, making them an easy (and pretty) investment for your sewing room.

Cracker Crumbs

My collection of vintage tins in rich, lush colors was the inspiration for this patchwork mini. To me, the blocks resemble little tins—some are full of "crackers" while others have been munched on! Whether totally full or half empty, these blocks are completely yummy.

MATERIALS

Yardage is based on a 42" usable width of fabric after prewashing and removing selvages.

- 8 chubby sixteenths (9" × 10½") of assorted cream prints for blocks
- ⅜ yard of wine print for blocks, inner border, and binding
- 1 fat quarter (18" × 21") of pink print for blocks and outer border
- 19 chubby sixteenths of assorted prints for blocks
- ¾ yard of fabric for backing
- 25" × 25" square of batting

CUTTING

Cut all pieces across the width of the fabric in the order given unless otherwise noted.

From the 8 assorted cream prints, cut a *combined* total of:

13 rectangles, 1⅛" × 2⅝"

25 squares, 2½" × 2½"; cut each square in half diagonally *once* to yield 2 triangles (combined total of 50)

From the pink print, cut:

4 strips, 2½" × 21"; crosscut into:
    2 strips, 2½" × 20½"
    2 strips, 2½" × 16½"

1 square, 2½" × 2½"; cut in half diagonally *once* to yield 2 triangles

Reserve the remainder of the pink print.

From the wine print, cut:

3 strips, 2½" × 42"; crosscut *1 of the strips* into 2 squares, 2½" × 2½". Cut each square in half diagonally *once* to yield 2 triangles (total of 4). Set aside the remainder of the cut strip, as well as the original 2 strips, for the binding (for my chubby-binding method provided on page 127, reduce the strip widths to 2").

2 strips, 1" × 42"; crosscut into:
    2 strips, 1" × 16½"
    2 strips, 1" × 15½"

Reserve the remainder of the wine print.

From the 19 assorted prints and the reserved remainder of the wine and pink prints, cut a *combined total* of:

60 rectangles, 1¼" × 2⅝"

16 rectangles, 1⅛" × 2⅝"

27 squares, 2½" × 2½"; cut each square in half diagonally *once* to yield 2 triangles (combined total of 54; grand total of 60 with previously cut wine and pink triangles)

PIECING THE BLOCKS

Sew all pieces with right sides together using a ¼" seam allowance. Press the seam allowances as indicated by the arrows or otherwise specified.

1. Choosing the prints randomly, select two assorted print 1¼" × 2⅝" rectangles and one cream 1⅛" × 2⅝" rectangle. Join a print rectangle to each long side of the cream rectangle. Press. Repeat to piece a total of 13 light units measuring 2⅝" square, including the seam allowances.

Make 13 light units,
2⅝" × 2⅝".

2. Again choosing the prints randomly, select two assorted print 1¼" × 2⅝" rectangles and one assorted print 1⅛" × 2⅝" rectangle. Join 1¼"-wide rectangles to each long side of the 1⅛"-wide rectangle. Press. Repeat

to piece a total of 12 dark units measuring 2⅝" square, including the seam allowances. Please note that you'll have 10 unused 1¼"-wide and four unused 1⅛"-wide assorted print rectangles; these have been included for added versatility as you piece the patchwork.

Make 12 dark units,
2⅝" × 2⅝".

3. Select a light unit from step 1. Join the long side of a cream 2½" triangle to the assorted print rectangle on opposite sides of the unit. Press. Trim away the dog-ear points.

 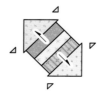

4. Repeat step 3 to join two assorted print 2½" triangles to the remaining sides of the light unit.

Staying Centered

To achieve accuracy in my patchwork when joining triangles to square or rectangular units, here's a trick that works beautifully. First, fold the long edge of the triangle in half, right sides together, and finger-press the center position to form a crease. Next, fold the edge of the unit the triangle will be joined to in half, also with right sides together, and finger-press that center position. Last, layer the pieces right sides together, aligning the center creases, and pin them in place for stitching. This quick step enables you to perfectly center the triangle onto the unit it will be joined to, which will tremendously increase the accuracy in your finished patchwork.

5. Using a rotary cutter and an acrylic ruler, measure ¼" out from the pieced point on each side of the block to trim away any excess fabric and bring the finished size of the block to 3½" square, including the seam allowances.

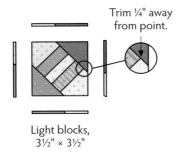

Trim ¼" away
from point.

Light blocks,
3½" × 3½"

6. Repeat steps 3–5 to piece a total of 13 light blocks.

7. Using the dark units from step 2 and the remaining cream and assorted print 2½" triangles, follow steps 3–5 to piece a total of 12 dark blocks measuring 3½" square, including the seam allowances. Please note that you'll have a handful of extra assorted print 2½" triangles; these have been included for added versatility as you piece the patchwork.

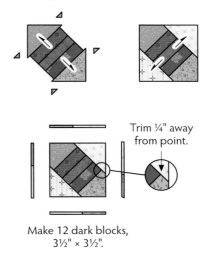

Trim ¼" away
from point.

Make 12 dark blocks,
3½" × 3½".

PIECING THE QUILT CENTER

1. Lay out three light blocks and two dark blocks in alternating positions, alternating the slant of the strips. Join the blocks. Press. Repeat to piece a total of three A rows measuring 3½" × 15½", including the seam allowances.

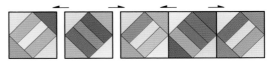

Make 3 A rows,
3½" × 15½".

2. Lay out three dark blocks and two light blocks in alternating positions, alternating the slant of the strips. Join the blocks. Press. Repeat to piece two B rows measuring 3½" × 15½", including the seam allowances.

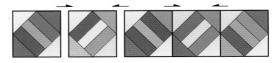

Make 2 B rows,
3½" × 15½".

Designed by Kim Diehl. Pieced by Jennifer Martinez. Machine quilted by Connie Tabor.

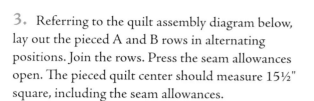

3. Referring to the quilt assembly diagram below, lay out the pieced A and B rows in alternating positions. Join the rows. Press the seam allowances open. The pieced quilt center should measure 15½" square, including the seam allowances.

ADDING THE BORDERS

1. Join a wine 1" × 15½" strip to the right and left sides of the quilt center. Press. Join a wine 1" × 16½" strip to each remaining side of the quilt center. Press.

2. Sew a pink 2½" × 16½" strip to the right and left sides of the quilt top. Press. Sew a pink 2½" × 20½" strip to each remaining side of the quilt top. Press.

COMPLETING THE QUILT

Layer and baste the quilt top, batting, and backing. Quilt the layers. The featured quilt was machine quilted with an edge-to-edge Baptist fan design. Join the wine binding strips to make one length and use it to bind the quilt.

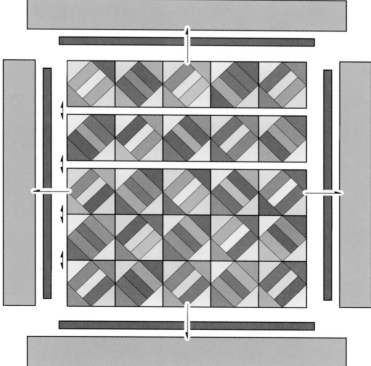

Quilt assembly

Cotton Blossoms

Break out your favorite prints and plaids and stitch up some fun with these Log Cabin blocks built from easily pieced skinny strips in a variety of lengths. Simple sprays of appliquéd blooms shine in the quilt center, leaving just the right amount of space to add some showstopping quilting.

MATERIALS

Yardage is based on a 42" usable width of fabric after prewashing and removing selvages. The featured project uses a combination of cotton prints and woven plaids, but any blend of fabrics that pleases you will work beautifully.

* 4 fat eighths (9" × 21") of assorted cream prints for blocks
* 1 fat eighth of red print A for blocks and border patchwork
* 1 fat eighth *each* of red and gold plaid for blocks and appliqués
* ⅓ yard of green plaid for blocks, appliqués, and border patchwork
* 1 fat quarter (18" × 21") of red print B for blocks and binding
* 20 chubby sixteenths (9" × 10½") of assorted prints and plaids for blocks and appliqués
* ⅞ yard of fabric for backing
* 29" × 29" square of batting
* Bias bar to make ¼"-wide stems
* Liquid glue for fabric, water-soluble and acid-free
* Fabric glue stick
* 4" × 5" rectangle of freezer paper
* Supplies for your favorite appliqué method

CUTTING

Cut all pieces across the width of the fabric in the order given unless otherwise noted. Refer to "Cutting Bias Strips" on page 119 to cut the bias strips. For greater ease, cutting instructions for the appliqués are provided separately.

From the 4 assorted cream prints, cut a *combined* total of:
4 rectangles, 1" × 1½"
4 rectangles, 1" × 2"
4 rectangles, 1" × 2½"
4 rectangles, 1" × 3"
4 rectangles, 1" × 3½"
4 rectangles, 1" × 4"
4 rectangles, 1" × 4½"
4 rectangles, 1" × 5"
4 rectangles, 1" × 5½"
4 rectangles, 1" × 6"
4 rectangles, 1" × 6½"
4 rectangles, 1" × 7"
4 rectangles, 1" × 7½"
4 rectangles, 1" × 8"
4 rectangles, 1" × 8½"
4 rectangles, 1" × 9"

From red print A, cut:
1 strip, 3½" × 21"; crosscut into 4 squares, 3½" × 3½".
   From the remainder of the strip, cut 4 squares,
      1½" × 1½", and 4 strips, 1" × 18½".
Reserve the remainder of red print A.

Continued on page 34

Continued from page 33

From the red plaid, cut:

1 strip, 3" × 12"

Reserve the remainder of the red plaid.

From the gold plaid, cut:

1 *bias* strip, 2" × 12"

Reserve the remainder of the gold plaid.

From the green plaid, cut:

2 strips, 2" × 42"; crosscut into 4 strips, 2" × 18½"

2 strips, 1½" × 42"; crosscut into 4 strips, 1½" × 18½"

Reserve the remainder of the green plaid.

From red print B, cut:

6 binding strips, 2½" × 21" (for my chubby-binding
    method provided on page 127, reduce the strip
    width to 2")

Reserve the remainder of red print B.

**From the 20 assorted prints and plaids, and the
remainder of all reserved prints and plaids
(excluding the green plaid), cut a *combined total* of:**

4 rectangles, 1" × 2"

4 rectangles, 1" × 2½"

4 rectangles, 1" × 3"

4 rectangles, 1" × 3½"

4 rectangles, 1" × 4"

4 rectangles, 1" × 4½"

4 rectangles, 1" × 5"

4 rectangles, 1" × 5½"

4 rectangles, 1" × 6"

4 rectangles, 1" × 6½"

4 rectangles, 1" × 7"

4 rectangles, 1" × 7½"

4 rectangles, 1" × 8"

4 rectangles, 1" × 8½"

4 rectangles, 1" × 9"

4 rectangles, 1" × 9½"

Reserve the scraps of all prints and plaids for
    the appliqués.

PIECING THE LOG CABIN BLOCKS

*Sew all pieces with right sides together using a ¼" seam
allowance. Press the seam allowances of all stitched
rectangles away from the red center square. As you stitch
the patchwork, please refer to the block illustration for
rectangle sizes and placement.*

1. Join a cream 1" × 1½" rectangle to one side of a red
A 1½" square. Press. Working in a counterclockwise
direction, join a cream 1" × 2" rectangle to the
adjacent side of the red square. Press. Continuing in
a counterclockwise direction, join a print 1" × 2"
rectangle to the adjacent side of the red square. Press.
Last, join a print 1" × 2½" rectangle to the remaining
side of the red square. Press.

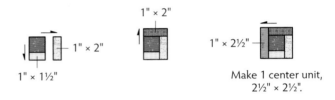

Make 1 center unit,
2½" × 2½".

EXTRA SNIPPET

Staying on Track

In the course of making scads of Log
Cabin projects, I've found that it can
sometimes be confusing where to add the
next rectangle as you piece the blocks. An
easy way to keep yourself on track is to
begin with the block illustration to stitch
the first row of rectangles around the
center square. Once the first row has been
completed and the pattern of color is
established, continue building the block,
always adding the next rectangle to the
side of the unit that contains two sewn
seams. This little trick will make it easy to
see where the next rectangle should be
added and help you avoid something we
all dislike the most—unsewing!

2. Continue working in a counterclockwise direction around the Log Cabin unit to build the block design by adding the remaining sizes of cream and assorted print rectangles, increasing the length of the rectangles as the size of the unit increases. The finished Log Cabin block should measure 9½" square, including the seam allowances.

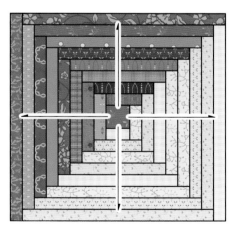

Make 4 Log Cabin blocks,
9½" × 9½".

3. Repeat steps 1 and 2 to piece a total of four Log Cabin blocks.

Piecing the Quilt Center

Lay out the four pieced Log Cabin blocks in two horizontal rows of two blocks. Join the blocks in each row. Press. Join the rows. Press The pieced quilt center should measure 18½" square, including the seam allowances.

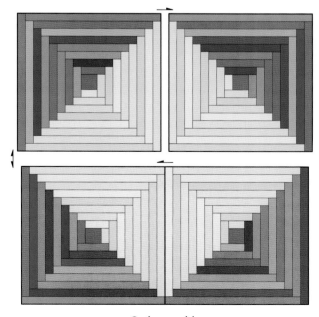

Quilt assembly

FINISHED QUILT SIZE: 24½" × 24½" ✦ FINISHED BLOCK SIZE: 9" × 9"

Designed and pieced by Kim Diehl. Machine quilted by Lois Walker.

ADDING THE APPLIQUÉS

Step-by-step instructions for my invisible machine-appliqué method begin on page 121, or you can substitute your own favorite method. Appliqué patterns for the flower, oak leaf, large and small leaves, and berry are provided on page 39.

1. Carefully join the red plaid strip and the gold plaid bias strip along the long edges, taking care not to stretch the fabric. Press the seam allowances toward the gold plaid.

2. Use your favorite method to prepare four flower appliqués from the pieced red-and-gold strip, aligning the marked line on the flower pattern with the seam line of the strip.

3. From the reserved remainder of the green plaid, cut four *bias* strips, 1" × 7". Referring to "Making Bias-Tube Stems and Vines" on page 123, stitch and prepare four stems. Apply a small amount of fabric glue stick to the seam allowance at the end of one stem. Turn the glued end under approximately ¼" so that the raw edge will be hidden from the front. Use a hot, dry iron to fuse the folded end in place. Repeat with each remaining stem.

4. Referring to the pictured quilt on page 36 for print choices (or creating your own blend of colors), use the reserved scraps of all fabrics to prepare the following appliqués:

- 4 oak leaves
- 4 large leaves
- 4 small leaves
- 12 berries

5. Fold the freezer-paper rectangle in half lengthwise, waxy sides together, and finger-press a center crease. Unfold the paper and use a pencil to trace the stem guide provided on page 39 onto the dull, nonwaxy side of one rectangle half. Refold the paper, waxy sides together, and use a hot, dry iron to fuse the layers. Cut out the stem guide on the drawn lines.

6. Referring to the appliqué placement guide below, lay out a flower, large leaf, and small leaf on one quadrant of the quilt center to begin forming the design. Position the stem guide onto the quilt top, curved edge out, placing it approximately ¼" in from the leaves. When you're happy with the arrangement, dot the quilt top next to the curved guide edge with liquid fabric glue at approximately ½" intervals. Position a prepared stem onto the quilt top along the glue-basted guide edge to perfectly shape it, with the finished end opposite the flower. Repeat with the remaining quadrants of the quilt center. Remove the stem guide.

7. Again referring to the appliqué placement guide, position an oak leaf along each stem, tucking the raw end under the stem approximately ¼" to prevent fraying. Pin or baste all leaves in place. Center and baste the flower over each raw stem end, again overlapping the pieces approximately ¼". Last, position and baste three berries along each stem. Using your favorite appliqué method, work from the bottom layer to the top to stitch the pieces in place.

Appliqué placement

PIECING AND ADDING THE BORDER

1. Join a red A 1" × 18½" strip to a green plaid 2" × 18½" strip along their long edges. Press. Join a green plaid 1½" × 18½" strip to the opposite edge of the red strip. Press. Repeat to piece a total of four border units measuring 3½" × 18½", including the seam allowances.

Make 4 border units, 3½" × 18½".

2. Using the quilt pictured on page 36 as a guide, join the narrow green edge of a border unit to the right and left sides of the quilt center. Press the seam allowances toward the border unit. Join a red A 3½" square to each end of the remaining border units. Press the seam allowances toward the border units. Join these pieced strips to the remaining sides of the quilt center. Press the seam allowances away from the quilt center.

COMPLETING THE QUILT

Layer and baste the quilt top, batting, and backing. Quilt the layers. The featured quilt was machine quilted with a curved feathered X in the quilt center, the appliqués were outlined to emphasize their shapes, and the remaining cream background area was filled in with free-form swirls. The darker "stair step" portions of each block were quilted with repeating diagonal lines, Xs were stitched onto the red block center squares, and a double X was stitched onto the red border corner squares. Last, the border units were quilted with serpentine feathers, including small strings of pearls in the center stems of the feathers. Join the red B binding strips to make one length and use it to bind the quilt.

Cotton Blossoms

Berry

Patterns do not include seam allowances.

Small leaf

Large leaf

Flower

Oak leaf

Stem guide

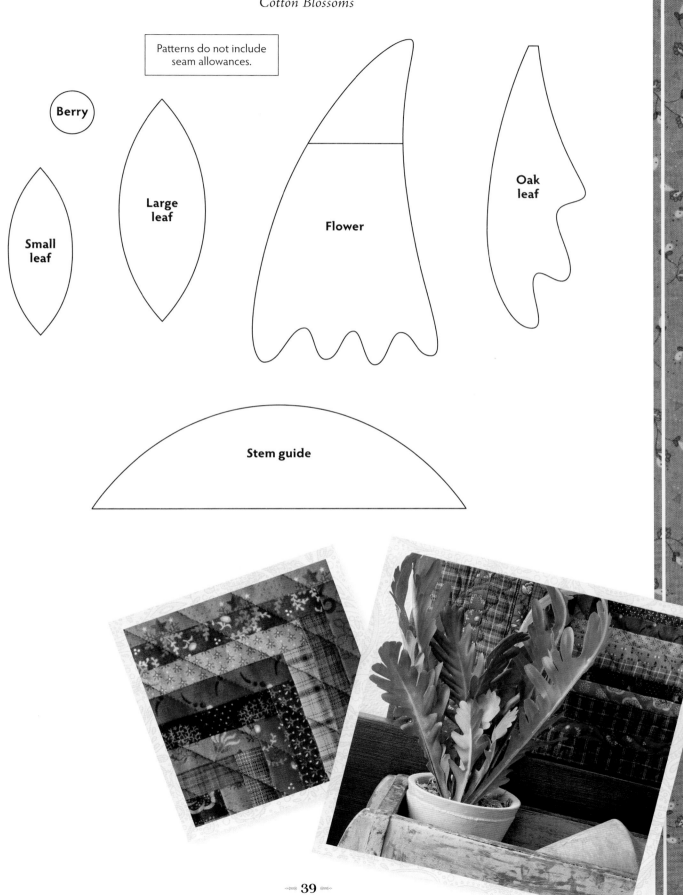

Skip to My Lou

Tiny aqua checkerboard squares look like little sprinkles of confetti when mingled among the "grownup" patchwork, and using a strip-set approach to piece them makes this task so approachable and doable. Scarlet stars complete the look and seal the deal!

MATERIALS

Yardage is based on a 42" usable width of fabric after prewashing and removing selvages.

+ ⅝ yard of aqua print for Checkerboard blocks and binding
+ ⅓ yard *each* of 4 assorted cream prints for blocks
+ 5 fat eighths (9" × 21") of assorted red prints for blocks
+ 19 charm squares (5" × 5") of assorted prints for blocks
+ ⅞ yard of fabric for backing
+ 30" × 30" square of batting

CUTTING

Before you begin cutting, please refer to the "Added Stability" tip on page 42. Cut all pieces across the width of the fabric in the order given unless otherwise noted.

From the aqua print, cut:

8 strips, 1" × 42"
1 strip, 1½" × 42"; crosscut into 16 squares, 1½" × 1½"
3 binding strips, 2½" × 42" (for my chubby-binding method on page 127, reduce the strip width to 2")

From *each* of the 4 assorted cream prints, cut:

2 strips, 1" × 42" (combined total of 8)
1 strip, 1½" × 42" (combined total of 4); crosscut into 16 squares, 1½" × 1½" (combined total of 64)
2 strips, 1¾" × 42" (combined total of 8); crosscut into 27 squares, 1¾" × 1¾" (combined total of 108)
Reserve the remainder of the assorted cream prints.

From the reserved remainder of the assorted cream prints, cut a *combined total* of:

18 squares, 2¼" × 2¼"; cut each square in half diagonally once to yield 2 triangles (combined total of 36)

From the 5 assorted red prints, cut a *combined total* of:

18 squares, 2¼" × 2¼"; cut each square in half diagonally *once* to yield 2 triangles (combined total of 36)
36 rectangles, 1¾" × 3"
Reserve the remainder of the 5 assorted red prints.

From *each* of the 19 assorted print charm squares and the reserved remainder of the 5 assorted red prints, cut:

8 squares, 1½" × 1½" (combined total of 192)

Note: *For added choices as you piece the patchwork, you may wish to cut an extra handful of 1½" squares.*

Added Stability

For added stability when working with the aqua and cream prints used for the small-scale patchwork in this quilt, I found it was worth taking a quick moment to add one preparation step. Before cutting the needed pieces from these fabrics, I lightly sprayed each one with Best Press (starch is another good alternative), and used a hot, dry iron to press them flat and remove any wrinkles. Applying Best Press gives the fabric a firm, almost paper-like texture, helping to produce more accurate results as you stitch the patchwork.

Piecing the Checkerboard Blocks

Sew all pieces with right sides together using a ¼" seam allowance. Press the seam allowances as indicated by the arrows or otherwise specified.

1. Join an aqua and a cream 1" × 42" strip along the long edges. Press. Repeat to piece a total of eight strip sets measuring 1½" × 42", including the seam allowances. Keep the strip sets organized by cream print. Crosscut the two strip sets sewn from each cream print into 64 segments, 1" × 1½" (combined total of 256).

Make 2 strip sets, 1½" × 42", from each cream print (8 total).
Cut 64 segments, 1" × 1½", from each print (256 total).

2. Choosing the cream prints randomly, join two strip-set segments to make a four-patch unit. Press. Repeat to piece a total of 128 four-patch units measuring 1½" square, including the seam allowances.

Make 128 units,
1½" × 1½".

3. Choosing the prints randomly, lay out eight four-patch units, 12 assorted print 1½" squares, four assorted cream 1½" squares, and one aqua 1½" square in five horizontal rows. Join the pieces in each row. Press. Join the rows. Press. Repeat to piece a total of 16 Checkerboard blocks measuring 5½" square, including the seam allowances.

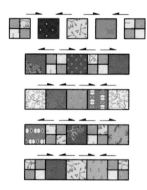 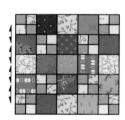

Make 16 Checkerboard blocks,
5½" × 5½".

Piecing the Star Blocks

1. Use a pencil and an acrylic ruler to draw a diagonal sewing line from corner to corner on the wrong side of 72 of the assorted cream 1¾" squares. Reserve the remaining cream 1¾" squares for later use.

2. Referring to the illustration on page 44, layer a prepared cream square onto one end of a red 1¾" × 3" rectangle. Stitch the pair together along the drawn line. Fold the resulting inner cream triangle open, aligning the corner with the corner of the rectangle. Press. Trim away the layers beneath the top triangle, leaving a ¼" seam allowance. In the same manner, use a second prepared cream 1¾" square to add a triangle to the remaining end of the red rectangle, orienting the drawn

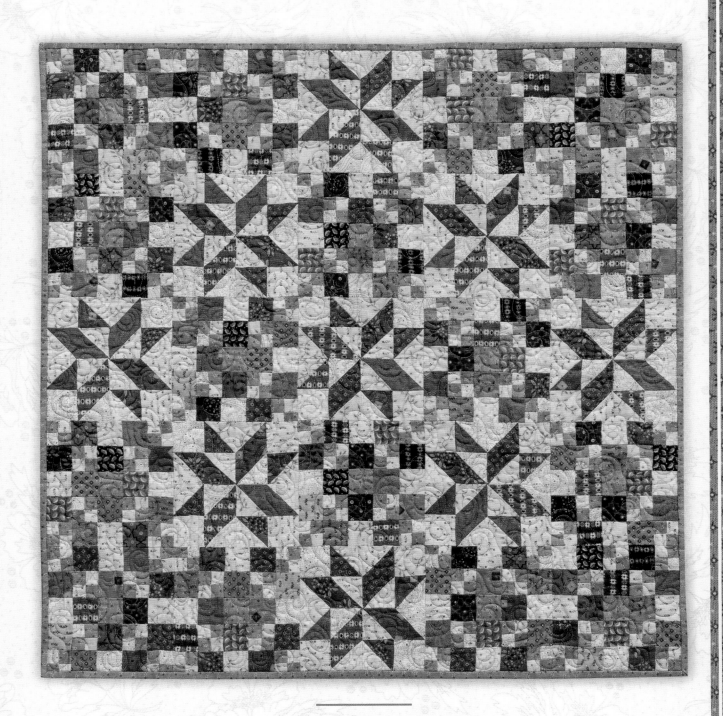

FINISHED QUILT SIZE: 25½" × 25½" • FINISHED BLOCK SIZE: 5" × 5"
Designed and pieced by Kim Diehl. Machine quilted by Connie Tabor.

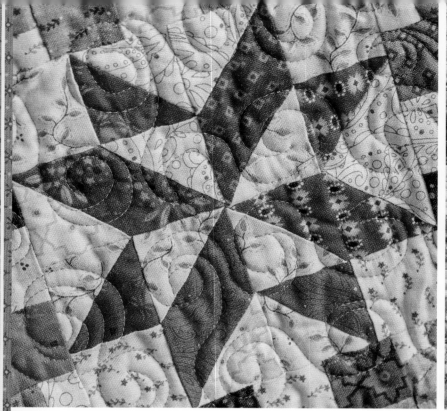

line as shown. Repeat to piece a total of 36 star-point units measuring 1¾" × 3", including the seam allowances.

Make 36 star-point units,
1¾" × 3".

3. Join a red and a cream 2¼" triangle along the long diagonal edges. Press. Trim away the dog-ear points. Repeat to piece a total of 36 half-square-triangle units measuring 1¾" square, including the seam allowances.

Make 36 half-square-triangle units,
1¾" × 1¾".

4. Join a cream 1¾" square to a half-square-triangle unit as shown. Press. Repeat to piece a total of 36 rectangles measuring 1¾" × 3", including the seam allowances.

Make 36 pieced rectangles,
1¾" × 3".

5. Join a pieced rectangle to a star-point unit from step 2. Press. Repeat to piece a total of 36 quarter units measuring 3" × 3", including the seam allowances.

Make 36 quarter units,
3" × 3".

6. Lay out four quarter units in two horizontal rows. Join the units in each row. Press. Join the rows. Press. Repeat to piece a total of nine Star blocks measuring 5½" square, including the seam allowances.

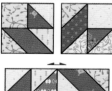

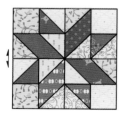

Make 9 Star blocks,
5½" × 5½".

PIECING THE QUILT TOP

1. Lay out four Checkerboard blocks and one Star block as shown. Join the blocks. Press. Repeat to piece a total of two A rows measuring 5½" × 25½", including the seam allowances.

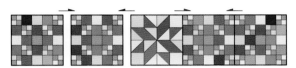

Make 2 of row A,
5½" × 25½".

2. Alternating the positions, lay out three Checkerboard blocks and two Star blocks. Join the blocks. Press. Repeat to piece two B rows measuring 5½" × 25½", including the seam allowances.

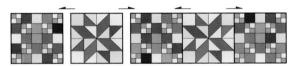

Make 2 of row B,
5½" × 25½".

3. Lay out three Star blocks and two Checkerboard blocks in alternating positions. Join the blocks. Press. The pieced C row should measure 5½" × 25½", including the seam allowances.

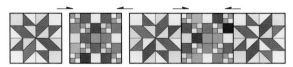

Make 1 of row C,
5½" × 25½".

4. Join the A, B, and C rows as shown in the quilt assembly diagram below. Press the seam allowances open.

COMPLETING THE QUILT

Layer and baste the quilt top, batting, and backing. Quilt the layers. The featured quilt was machine quilted with an edge-to-edge free-form pattern of swirls and circles. Join the aqua binding strips to make one length and use it to bind the quilt.

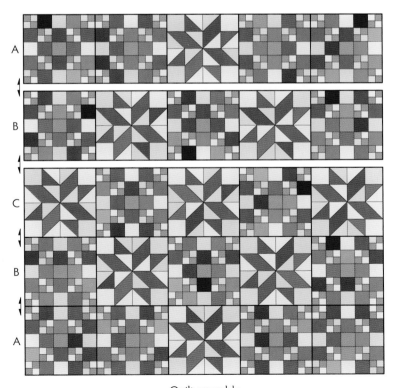

Quilt assembly

Double Dutch Stars

Two-color quilts are so striking and among my favorites to stitch, because using fewer prints simplifies the preparation steps and produces quick progress when cutting. Most of all, these pieced stars in saturated shades of midnight blue are a breeze to sew and a joy to live with.

MATERIALS

Yardage is based on a 42" usable width of fabric after prewashing and removing selvages.

* 4 chubby sixteenths (9" × 10½") of assorted cream prints for blocks
* 1 chubby sixteenth of medium-dark blue print for blocks
* ⅜ yard of dark blue print A for star center squares and binding
* ¼ yard (not a fat quarter) of dark blue print B for star points and border
* ½ yard of fabric for backing
* 15" × 31" rectangle of batting

CUTTING

Cut all pieces across the width of the fabric in the order given unless otherwise noted.

From the 4 cream prints, cut a *combined total of:*
18 squares, 2⅞" × 2⅞"; cut each square in half diagonally *once* to yield 2 triangles (combined total of 36)
12 squares, 2½" × 2½"

From the medium-dark blue print, cut:
4 strips, 1½" × 10½"; crosscut into 24 squares, 1½" × 1½"

From dark blue print A, cut:
3 strips, 2½" × 42" (for my chubby-binding method provided on page 127, reduce the strip width to 2")
3 squares, 4½" × 4½"
6 squares, 2⅞" × 2⅞"; cut each square in half diagonally *once* to yield 2 triangles (total of 12)

From dark blue print B, cut:
1 strip, 2⅞" × 42"; crosscut into 12 squares, 2⅞" × 2⅞". Cut each square in half diagonally *once* to yield 2 triangles (total of 24).
2 strips, 1½" × 42"; crosscut into:
   2 strips, 1½" × 26½"
   2 strips, 1½" × 8½"

PIECING THE STAR BLOCKS

Sew all pieces with right sides together using a ¼" seam allowance. Press the seam allowances as indicated by the arrows or otherwise specified.

1. Using a pencil and an acrylic ruler, draw a diagonal sewing line from corner to corner on the wrong side of each cream 2½" square and each medium-dark blue 1½" square. Reserve the prepared blue squares for later.

2. Layer a prepared cream 2½" square onto two opposite corners of a dark blue A 4½" square. Stitch the layered cream squares along the drawn diagonal lines. Fold the resulting cream triangles open, aligning the corners with the corners of the blue square. Trim away the layers beneath the top triangles, leaving ¼" seam allowances. In the same manner, use two additional prepared cream 2½" squares to add cream triangles to the remaining corners of the blue square. Repeat to piece a total of three square-in-a-square units measuring 4½" square, including the seam allowances.

Make 3 square-in-a-square units, 4½" × 4½".

3. Join a cream and a dark blue B 2⅞" triangle along the long diagonal edges. Press. Trim away the dog-ear points. Repeat to piece 24 half-square-triangle units from the dark blue B print and 12 half-square-triangle units from the dark blue A print, all measuring 2½" square, including the seam allowances. Keep the units organized by print.

Make 24 units, 2½" × 2½". Make 12 units, 2½" × 2½".

4. Layer a reserved prepared medium-dark blue 1½" square onto the cream corner of a dark blue B half-square-triangle unit. Stitch, press, and trim as previously instructed. Repeat to piece a total of 24 units measuring 2½" square, including the seam allowances.

Make 24 units, 2½" × 2½".

5. Join two units from step 4. Press. Repeat to piece a total of 12 star-point units measuring 2½" × 4½", including the seam allowances.

Make 12 units,
2½" × 4½".

6. Lay out one square-in-a-square unit, four dark blue A half-square-triangle units, and four star-point units in three horizontal rows. Join the pieces in each row. Press. Join the rows. Press. Repeat to piece a total of three Star blocks measuring 8½" square, including the seam allowances.

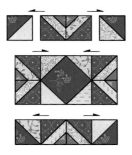
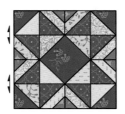

Star block,
8½" × 8½".

PIECING THE TABLE RUNNER

1. Using the table runner pictured as a guide, lay out and join the three Star blocks. Press the seam allowances open. The pieced quilt center should measure 8½" × 24½", including the seam allowances.

2. Join a dark blue B 1½" × 8½" rectangle to each short end of the table-runner center. Join a dark blue B 1½" × 26½" strip to each remaining side of the table-runner center. Press all seam allowances toward the borders.

COMPLETING THE TABLE RUNNER

Layer and baste the table-runner top, batting, and backing. Quilt the layers. The featured table runner was machine quilted with an edge-to-edge diagonal crosshatch design. Join the dark blue A binding strips to make one length and use it to bind the runner.

FINISHED TABLE-RUNNER SIZE: 10½" × 26½"
FINISHED BLOCK SIZE: 8" × 8"
Designed and pieced by Kim Diehl.
Machine quilted by Deborah Poole.

Chicken Scratch Patch

Three humble yet long-favored patchwork blocks—Pinwheel, Nine Patch, and Hourglass—join forces beautifully in this small but sassy quilt. Snippets of colorful prints mix and match easily into these traditional blocks, and a framework of warm chocolate brown is the ideal finishing touch.

MATERIALS

+ 4 fat eighths (9" × 21") of assorted cream prints for blocks and border patchwork
+ 1 fat quarter of brown print A for blocks and border patchwork
+ 1 fat eighth of brown print B for blocks and border patchwork
+ 1 fat quarter (18" × 21") of red print for blocks and binding
+ 15 squares, 6" × 6", of assorted prints for blocks
+ 1 fat quarter of fabric for backing
+ 19" × 21" rectangle of batting

CUTTING

Cut all pieces across the width of the fabric in the order given unless otherwise noted.

From *each* of the 4 assorted cream prints, cut:
1 strip, 3¼" × 21"; crosscut into 4 squares, 3¼" × 3¼" (combined total of 16). Cut each square in half diagonally *twice* to yield 4 triangles (combined total of 64).
1 strip, 1" × 21"; crosscut into 11 rectangles, 1" × 1½" (combined total of 44)
1 strip, 1½" × 21"; crosscut into:
    5 squares, 1½" × 1½" (combined total of 20)
    1 rectangle, 1½" × 2½" (combined total of 4)

From brown print A, cut:
2 strips, 3¼" × 21"; crosscut into 7 squares, 3¼" × 3¼". Cut each square in half diagonally *twice* to yield 4 triangles (total of 28).
2 strips, 1½" × 21"; crosscut into:
    6 rectangles, 1½" × 2½"
    4 squares, 1½" × 1½"
Keep the pieces organized by print. Reserve the remainder of the brown A print.

From brown print B, cut:
2 strips, 3¼" × 21"; crosscut into 7 squares, 3¼" × 3¼". Cut each square in half diagonally *twice* to yield 4 triangles (total of 28).
1 strip, 1½" × 21"; crosscut into 4 rectangles, 1½" × 2½"
Keep the pieces organized by print. Reserve the remainder of the brown B print.

Continued on page 52

Continued from page 51

From the red print, cut:

4 binding strips, 2½" × 21" (for my chubby-binding method provided on page 127, reduce the strip width to 2")

Reserve the remainder of the red print.

From the 15 assorted prints, the reserved remainder of brown prints A and B, and the reserved remainder of the red print, cut a *combined total* of:

40 squares, 1⅞" × 1⅞", in matching sets of 2 from each chosen print, for the Pinwheel blocks; cut each square in half diagonally *once* to yield 2 triangles (combined total of 80). Keep the triangles organized by print.

88 squares, 1" × 1", for the Nine Patch Variation blocks. For added choices as you stitch the patchwork, you may wish to cut a handful of extra squares.

PIECING THE PINWHEEL BLOCKS

Sew all pieces with right sides together using a ¼" seam allowance. Press the seam allowances as indicated by the arrows or otherwise specified.

1. Select one set of four triangles cut from a single print, and a second set of four triangles cut from a complementary print. Join two triangles (one from each print) along the long diagonal edges. Press. Trim away the dog-ear points. Repeat to piece a total of four half-square-triangle units measuring 1½" square, including the seam allowances.

Make 4 half-square-triangle units,
1½" × 1½".

2. Lay out the four half-square-triangle units in two horizontal rows as shown. Join the units in each row. Press. Join the rows. Press. The pieced Pinwheel block should measure 2½" square, including the seam allowances.

Pinwheel block,
2½" × 2½"

3. Repeat steps 1 and 2 to piece a total of 10 Pinwheel blocks.

PIECING THE NINE PATCH VARIATION BLOCKS

1. Choosing the prints randomly, lay out four assorted 1" squares in two horizontal rows. Join the squares in each row. Press. Join the rows. Press. Repeat to piece a total of 11 four-patch units measuring 1½" square, including the seam allowances.

Make 11 four-patch units,
1½" × 1½".

2. Lay out four assorted 1" squares, four assorted cream 1" × 1½" rectangles, and one four-patch unit in three horizontal rows as shown. Join the pieces in each row. Press. Join the rows. Press. The pieced Nine Patch Variation block should measure 2½" square, including the seam allowances.

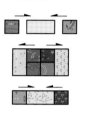

Nine Patch Variation,
2½" × 2½"

3. Repeat steps 1 and 2 to piece a total of 11 Nine Patch Variation blocks.

PIECING THE HOURGLASS BLOCKS

1. Select a brown print A and a cream triangle. Join, press, and trim as previously instructed. Repeat to piece a total of 28 brown A triangle units and make 28 brown B triangle units. Please note that the remaining eight cream triangles will be unused.

Make 28 each.

2. Join a brown A and a brown B triangle unit as shown. Press. Trim away the dog-ear points. Repeat to piece a total of 28 Hourglass blocks measuring 2½" square, including the seam allowances.

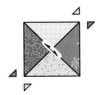

Make 28 Hourglass blocks, 2½" × 2½".

PIECING THE QUILT TOP

1. Lay out four Hourglass blocks, two Nine Patch Variation blocks, and one Pinwheel block as shown. Join the pieces. Press. Repeat to piece a total of four A rows measuring 2½" × 14½", including the seam allowances.

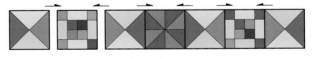

Make 4 of row A, 2½" × 14½".

2. Lay out four Hourglass blocks, two Pinwheel blocks, and one Nine Patch Variation block as shown. Join the pieces. Press. Repeat to piece a total of three B rows measuring 2½" × 14½", including the seam allowances.

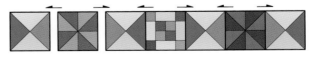

Make 3 of row B, 2½" × 14½".

FINISHED QUILT SIZE: 14½" × 16½" • FINISHED BLOCK SIZE: 2" × 2"

Designed and pieced by Kim Diehl. Machine quilted by Rebecca Silbaugh.

3. Referring to the quilt assembly diagram, lay out the A and B rows in alternating positions. Join the rows. Press. The pieced quilt top should measure 14½" square, including the seam allowances.

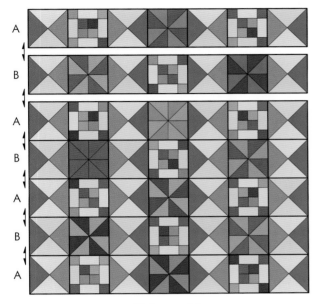

Quilt assembly

PIECING AND ADDING THE BORDER

1. Use a pencil and an acrylic ruler to draw a diagonal sewing line from corner to corner on the wrong side of each cream 1½" square. Repeat with the brown A 1½" squares. Set aside the prepared brown A squares for later use.

2. Layer a prepared cream 1½" square onto one end of a brown A or B rectangle. Stitch the pair together along the drawn line. Fold the resulting inner cream triangle open, aligning the corner with the corner of the brown rectangle. Press. Trim away the layers beneath the top triangle, leaving a ¼" seam allowance. In the same manner, add a mirror-image cream triangle to the remaining end of the brown rectangle to form a flying-geese unit measuring 1½" × 2½", including the

seam allowances. Repeat to piece a total of six brown A and four brown B flying-geese units.

Make 6 A units,
1½" × 2½".   Make 4 B units,
1½" × 2½".

3. Using the reserved prepared brown A 1½" squares and the cream 1½" × 2½" rectangles, follow step 2 to piece two half-flying-geese units and two mirror-image half-flying-geese units, each measuring 1½" × 2½", including the seam allowances.

Make 2 of each unit,
1½" × 2½".

4. Lay out three brown A flying-geese units and two brown B flying-geese units from step 3, one half-flying-geese unit, and one mirror-image half-flying-geese unit as shown. Join the units. Press. Repeat to piece a total of two border strips measuring 1½" × 14½", including the seam allowances.

Make 2 top/bottom border strips,
1½" × 14½".

5. Using the pictured quilt as a guide, join the border strips to the top and bottom edges of the quilt top. Press the seam allowances open.

COMPLETING THE QUILT

Layer and baste the quilt top, batting, and backing. Quilt the layers. The featured quilt was machine quilted with an edge-to-edge orange-peel design. Join the red binding strips to make one length and use it to bind the quilt.

Hickory Dickory

Seeing stars can sometimes be a good thing, especially when they're pieced and patched from your favorite prints! This mini brings all the good feels from start to finish—stitching the simply pieced stars, strips, and checkerboard, and then living with the colorful fruits of your labor.

MATERIALS

Yardage is based on a 42" usable width of fabric after prewashing and removing selvages.

- 8 chubby sixteenths (9" × 10½") of assorted cream prints for Star blocks and checkerboard border
- 1 fat quarter (18" × 21") of black print for checkerboard border and binding
- 6 chubby sixteenths of assorted prints for Star blocks and checkerboard border
- 1 chubby sixteenth of chestnut print for Star blocks, border strips, and checkerboard border
- 13 chubby sixteenths of assorted prints for border strips and checkerboard border
- ⅔ yard of fabric for backing
- 23" × 27" rectangle of batting

CUTTING

Cut all pieces across the width of the fabric in the order given unless otherwise noted.

From the 8 assorted cream prints, cut a *combined* total of:
24 rectangles, 1½" × 2½"
36 squares, 1½" × 1½"
8 squares, 1⅞" × 1⅞"; cut each square in half diagonally *once* to yield 2 triangles (total of 16)

From *each* of the 6 assorted prints chosen for the Star blocks, cut:
8 squares, 1½" × 1½" (combined total of 48)
1 square, 2½" × 2½" (combined total of 6)
Keep the squares organized by print for the star sets.
    Reserve the assorted print scraps.

From the chestnut print, cut:
1 strip, 1⅞" × 10½"; crosscut into 4 squares, 1⅞" × 1⅞". Cut each square in half diagonally *once* to yield 2 triangles (total of 8).
Reserve the chestnut print scraps.

From the 13 assorted prints for the border strips and the reserved scraps of the 6 assorted Star block prints and chestnut print, cut a *combined total* of:
2 strips, 1½" × 8½" (border 1)
10 sets of 2 matching strips, 1½" × 10½" (borders 1, 3, and 5)
120 squares, 1½" × 1½"

From the black print, cut:
1 strip, 1½" × 21"; crosscut into 9 squares, 1½" × 1½" (grand total of 129 with previously cut squares)
5 binding strips, 2½" × 21" (for my chubby-binding method provided on page 127, reduce the strip width to 2")

PIECING THE STAR BLOCKS

Sew all pieces with right sides together using a ¼" seam allowance. Press the seam allowances as indicated by the arrows or otherwise specified.

1. Join a cream and a chestnut 1⅞" triangle along the long diagonal edges. Press. Trim away the dog-ear points. Repeat, using each cream print once, to piece a total of eight chestnut half-square-triangle units measuring 1½" square, including the seam allowances. Please note that the remaining eight cream triangles will be unused.

Make 8 units,
1½" × 1½".

2. Select a set of star squares cut from a single print, four cream 1½" × 2½" rectangles, three cream 1½" squares, and one chestnut half-square-triangle unit from step 1. Use a pencil and an acrylic ruler to draw a diagonal sewing line from corner to corner on the wrong side of the eight star print 1½" squares.

3. Layer a prepared star print 1½" square onto one end of a cream 1½" × 2½" rectangle. Join the pair along the drawn line. Fold the resulting inner triangle open, aligning the corner with the corner of the cream rectangle. Press. Trim away the layers beneath the top triangle, leaving a ¼" seam allowance. In the same manner, add a mirror-image triangle to the remaining end of the rectangle. Repeat to piece a total of four star-point units measuring 1½" × 2½", including the seam allowances.

Make 4 star-point units,
1½" × 2½".

4. Lay out the four star-point units, three cream 1½" squares, the star print 2½" square, and one chestnut half-square-triangle unit in three horizontal rows as shown. Join the pieces in each row. Press. Join the rows. Press. The pieced Star block A should measure 4½" square, including the seam allowances.

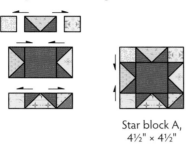

Star block A,
4½" × 4½"

5. Repeat steps 2–4 to piece a total of four of Star block A.

6. Using the remaining two sets of star squares, the cream 1½" × 2½" rectangles, the cream 1½" squares, and the remaining chestnut half-square-triangle units, follow steps 2–4 to piece two of Star block B as shown. (Please note that each Star block B uses two cream 1½" squares and two chestnut half-square-triangle units for the block corners.) Each block should measure 4½" square, including the seam allowances.

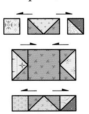

Star block B,
4½" × 4½"

PIECING THE QUILT CENTER

Lay out the blocks in three horizontal rows of two blocks. Press. Join the rows. Press. The pieced quilt center should measure 8½" × 12½", including the seam allowances.

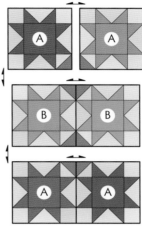

Quilt assembly

PIECING AND ADDING THE BORDERS

1. Select the matching pairs of 1½" × 10½" strips cut for borders 1, 3, and 5. Join each pair to make one long strip. Press the seam allowances open. From the 10 resulting pieced strips, refer to the adding the borders diagram on page 61 to cut:

- 4 strips, 1½" × 12½"
- 4 strips, 1½" × 16½"
- 2 strips, 1½" × 20½"

2. Using the assorted print 1½" squares cut for the checkerboard border, sew the squares end to end, pressing the seam allowances to one side, to make the following:

- 2 strips, 1½" × 10½" (10 squares per strip)
- 4 strips, 1½" × 14½" (14 squares per strip)
- 2 strips, 1½" × 18½" (18 squares per strip)

Please note that you'll have 17 unused squares; these have been included for added versatility as you piece the borders.

FINISHED QUILT SIZE: 18½" × 22½" ✦ FINISHED BLOCK SIZE: 4" × 4"
Designed and pieced by Kim Diehl. Machine quilted by Connie Tabor.

3. Referring to the border diagram for strip sizes, join a 1½" × 12½" strip to the right and left sides of the quilt center. Press. Join a cream 1½" square to each end of the two 1½" × 8½" strips. Press. Join these pieced strips to the top and bottom edges of the quilt center. Press. Continue working from the center outward to add and press the border strips.

COMPLETING THE QUILT

Layer and baste the quilt top, batting, and backing. Quilt the layers. The featured quilt was machine quilted with an edge-to-edge Baptist Fan design. Join the black binding strips to make one length and use it to bind the quilt.

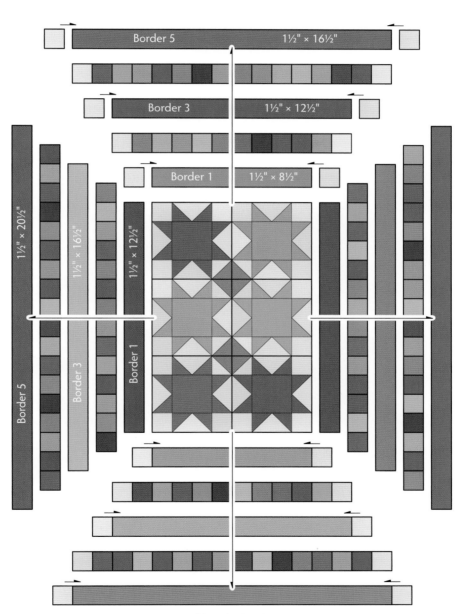

Adding the borders

Esther's Garden Box

It's been said that a picture is worth a thousand words, and the same can be said for quilts! Inspired by memories of my grandma Esther, the prints and colors she favored, and her hand-pieced quilts, this charming mini sums up her quietly remarkable spirit without a single spoken word.

Finished quilt size: 14½" × 14½"
Finished block sizes:
    Center block: 6" × 6"
    Pinwheel blocks: 2" × 2"

Designed, pieced, machine appliquéd,
and hand quilted by Kim Diehl.

Materials

+ 8 chubby sixteenths (9" × 10½") of assorted cream prints for appliqués and Pinwheel blocks
+ 1 fat quarter (18" × 21") of brown print for appliqués and binding
+ 4 chubby sixteenths of assorted prints (collectively referred to as "dark") for appliqués and Pinwheel blocks
+ 16 charm squares (5" × 5") of assorted prints (collectively referred to as "dark") for Pinwheel blocks
+ 1 fat quarter of fabric for backing
+ 19" × 19" square of batting
+ Supplies for your favorite appliqué method

Cutting

Cut all pieces across the width of the fabric in the order given. For greater ease, cutting instructions for the appliqués are provided separately.

From *each* of the 8 assorted cream prints, cut:

1 strip, 3⅞" × 10½"; crosscut into 1 square, 3⅞" × 3⅞" (combined total of 8). Cut each square in half diagonally *once* to yield 2 triangles (combined total of 16).

2 strips, 1⅞" × 10½"; crosscut into 10 squares, 1⅞" × 1⅞" (combined total of 80). Cut each square in half diagonally *once* to yield 2 triangles (combined total of 160). Keep the triangles organized by print.

From the brown print, cut:

4 binding strips, 2½" × 21" (for my chubby-binding method provided on page 127, reduce the strip width to 2")

Reserve the remainder of the brown print for the appliqués.

From *each* of the 4 dark print chubby sixteenths, cut:

1 strip, 1⅞" × 10½"; crosscut into 4 squares, 1⅞" × 1⅞" (combined total of 16). Cut each square in half diagonally *once* to yield 2 triangles (combined total of 32). Keep the triangles organized by print.

Reserve the remainder of the dark prints for the appliqués.

From *each* of the 16 dark print charm squares, cut:

4 squares, 1⅞" × 1⅞" (combined total of 64); cut each square in half diagonally once to yield 2 triangles (combined total of 128; grand total of 160 with previously cut dark 1⅞" triangles). Keep the triangles organized by print.

PIECING AND APPLIQUÉING THE CENTER BLOCK

Sew all pieces with right sides together using a ¼" seam allowance. Press the seam allowances as indicated by the arrows or otherwise specified. Step-by-step instructions for my invisible machine-appliqué method begin on page 121, or you can substitute your own favorite method. Appliqué patterns for the center block are provided on page 67.

1. Select one 3⅞" triangle from each of the eight cream prints. The remaining eight cream triangles will be unused.

2. Join two cream triangles along the long diagonal edges. Press. Trim away the dog-ear points. Repeat to piece a total of four cream half-square-triangle units measuring 3½" square, including the seam allowances.

Make 4 units,
3½" × 3½".

3. Lay out the cream half-square-triangle units in two horizontal rows. Join the units in each row. Press. Join the rows. Press. (Pressing all block seams open will help form a smooth foundation for the appliqué design.) The pieced cream pinwheel unit should measure 6½" square, including the seam allowances.

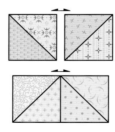
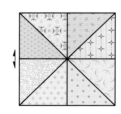

Make 1 cream pinwheel unit,
6½" × 6½".

4. Using your favorite appliqué method and the remainder of the brown and dark prints, prepare:

- 1 swag
- 1 stem unit
- 4 bud bases
- 4 leaves
- 4 leaves reversed
- 4 bud centers

5. Referring to the appliqué placement guide below and using the seams as built-in registration points to evenly space and position the appliqués, work from the bottom layer to the top to arrange the design on the cream pinwheel unit from step 3. When you're pleased with the placement, pin or baste the appliqués in place. Work from the bottom layer to the top to stitch the design.

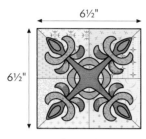

Appliqué placement

PIECING THE PINWHEEL BLOCKS

1. Select four matching cream 1⅞" triangles and four matching dark 1⅞" triangles. Join a cream and a dark triangle along the long diagonal edges. Press. Trim away the dog-ear points. Repeat to piece a total of four cream-and-dark half-square-triangle units measuring 1½" square, including the seam allowances.

Make 4 units,
1½" × 1½".

2. Lay out the half-square-triangle units in two horizontal rows as shown. Join the units in each row. Press. Join the rows. Press. The pieced Pinwheel block should measure 2½" square, including the seam allowances.

Pinwheel block,
2½" × 2½"

3. Repeat steps 1 and 2 to piece a total of 40 Pinwheel blocks.

PIECING THE QUILT TOP

1. Lay out seven Pinwheel blocks end to end. Join the blocks. Press. Repeat to piece a total of four long pinwheel rows measuring 2½" × 14½", including the seam allowances.

Make 4 long pinwheel rows,
2½" × 14½".

2. Lay out six Pinwheel blocks in three horizontal rows of two blocks. Join the blocks in each row. Press. Join the rows. Press. Repeat to piece a total of two side pinwheel sections measuring 4½" × 6½", including the seam allowances.

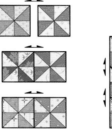

Make 2 side pinwheel sections,
4½" × 6½".

3. Referring to the quilt assembly diagram on page 66, join a side pinwheel section to the right and left sides of the appliquéd center block. Press.

4. Sew two long pinwheel rows from step 1 together along the long edges. Press. Repeat for a total of two joined pinwheel rows measuring 4½" × 14½", including the seam allowances. Sew these joined pinwheel rows to the top and bottom edges of the center block unit. Press.

COMPLETING THE QUILT

Layer and baste the quilt top, batting, and backing. Quilt the layers. The featured quilt was hand quilted in the big-stitch method as described in "Big-Stitch Hand Quilting" on page 126, with the blocks stitched in the ditch (along the seam lines), and the appliqués outlined to emphasize their shapes. Join the brown binding strips to make one length and use it to bind the quilt.

Quilt assembly

Framed and Fabulous

Don't let your small unused orphan blocks languish in a drawer—put them to good use and give them another chance to shine! My favorite way to do this is to choose an interesting wooden picture frame (I like the look of a square frame with about an 8" to 10" opening, but any frame you choose will work well) and remove the glass insert and backing pieces. Use the backing piece and a black marker to transfer the square or rectangle shape to a piece of chicken wire (small sheets of chicken wire can be purchased in craft stores or from online retailers). Cut the chicken wire along the inside of the drawn lines using a wire cutter. Anchor the chicken wire to the back side of the frame opening with a staple gun (a hot glue gun will also work, perhaps with the wire a bit more delicately attached). Use small clothespins to clip orphan blocks, or even a mini-quilt, to the chicken wire. Patchwork blocks can be changed and rotated throughout the year to reflect the seasons or special holidays. These little framed bits of quilted art also make great gifts!

Esther's Garden Box

Patterns do not include
seam allowances.

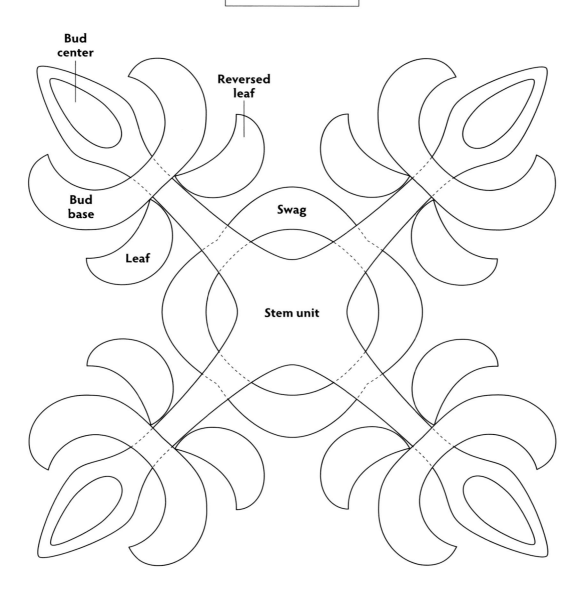

Bud center

Reversed leaf

Bud base

Swag

Leaf

Stem unit

Fair and Square

Tiny pieced blocks can be the showiest when given the chance to shine! Small-scale patchwork means there's less room for mistakes to hide, but I've learned to embrace any less-than-perfect blocks—they add quirky charm and show determination to finish.

___

MATERIALS

+ 4" × 4" square *each* of 3 assorted aqua, 1 teal, and 4 assorted dark red prints for blocks
+ 4" × 5" rectangle of medium red print for blocks
+ 4" × 10" rectangle *each* of 3 assorted cream prints for blocks
+ 1 chubby sixteenth (9" × 10½") of teal print for blocks and binding
+ 3½" × 8½" rectangle of aqua print for border
+ 6" × 8" rectangle of dark red print for border
+ 11" × 11" square of fabric for backing
+ 11" × 11" square of batting

CUTTING

Cut all pieces across the width of the fabric in the order given unless otherwise noted.

From *each* of the aqua, teal, and dark red squares and the teal chubby sixteenth, cut:
3 rectangles, 1" × 3" (combined total of 27)
Keep the pieces organized by print. Reserve the remainder of the teal chubby sixteenth.

From the medium red print, cut:
4 rectangles, 1" × 3"

From 1 cream print, cut:
8 rectangles, 1" × 3"
Keep the rectangles organized by print for the red blocks.

From a different cream print, cut:
9 rectangles, 1" × 3"
Keep the rectangles organized by print for the aqua blocks.

From the remaining cream print, cut:
6 rectangles, 1" × 3"
Keep the rectangles organized by print for the teal blocks.

From the aqua print for the border, cut:
2 rectangles, ¾" × 5½"
2 rectangles, ¾" × 7½"

From the dark red print for the border, cut:
2 rectangles, 1¼" × 5½"
2 rectangles, 1¼" × 7½"

From the reserved remainder of the teal chubby sixteenth, cut:
4 binding strips, 1¾" × 10½"

PIECING THE AQUA AND TEAL NINE PATCH BLOCKS

Sew all pieces with right sides together using a ¼" seam allowance. Press the seam allowances as indicated by the arrows or otherwise specified.

1. Select one set of three matching aqua 1" × 3" rectangles and three of the cream 1" × 3" rectangles cut for the aqua blocks. Join an aqua rectangle to each long side of a cream rectangle to make an outer-row strip set measuring 2" × 3", including the seam allowances. Press. Crosscut the strip set into two segments, 1" × 2". Join a cream rectangle to each long side of an aqua rectangle to make a middle-row strip set measuring 2" × 3", including the seam allowances. Press. Crosscut the strip set into one segment 1" × 2".

Make 1 strip set, 2" × 3".
Cut 2 segments, 1" × 2".

Make 1 strip set, 2" × 3".
Cut 1 segment, 1" × 2".

2. Lay out the two outer-row segments and the middle-row segment in three horizontal rows. Join the rows. Press. The pieced block should measure 2" square, including the seam allowances. Repeat to piece a total of three aqua Nine Patch blocks.

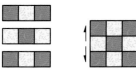

Make 3 aqua blocks total,
2" × 2".

3. Repeat steps 1 and 2 using the teal and cream rectangle sets to piece a total of two teal Nine Patch blocks that measure 2" square.

Make 2 teal blocks,
2" × 2".

Fair and Square

FINISHED QUILT SIZE: 7" × 7" • FINISHED BLOCK SIZE: 1½" × 1½"
Designed, pieced, and hand quilted by Kim Diehl.

PIECING THE RED NINE PATCH BLOCKS

1. Select one set of three matching dark red 1" × 3" rectangles, one medium red 1" × 3" rectangle, and two of the cream 1" × 3" rectangles cut for the red blocks. Join a cream rectangle to each long side of a dark red rectangle to make an outer-row strip set. Press and crosscut as before to make two segments, 1" × 2". Join a dark red rectangle to each long side of a medium red rectangle to make a middle-row strip set. Press and crosscut the strip set into one segment, 1" × 2".

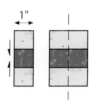 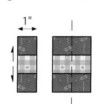

Make 1 strip set, 2" × 3".
Cut 2 segments, 1" × 2".

Make 1 strip set, 2" × 3".
Cut 1 segment, 1" × 2".

2. Lay out the two outer-row segments and the middle-row segment in three horizontal rows. Join the rows. Press. The block should measure 2" square, including the seam allowances. Repeat using the remaining dark red, medium red, and cream rectangle sets to make a total of four red Nine Patch blocks.

Make 4 blocks,
2" × 2".

PIECING THE QUILT CENTER

Referring to the quilt assembly diagram, lay out the aqua, teal, and red Nine Patch blocks in three horizontal rows. Join the blocks in each row. Press. Join the rows. Press. The pieced quilt center should measure 5" square, including the seam allowances.

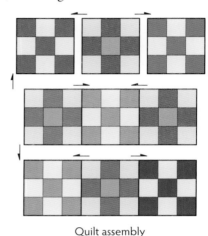

Quilt assembly

PIECING AND ADDING THE BORDER

1. Join an aqua ¾" × 5½" rectangle and a dark red 1¼" × 5½" rectangle along the long edges. Press. Trim the pieced unit to 5" long. Repeat to piece and trim a total of two border units. In the same manner, join, press, and trim the remaining aqua and dark red rectangles to make two pieced border units measuring 7" long.

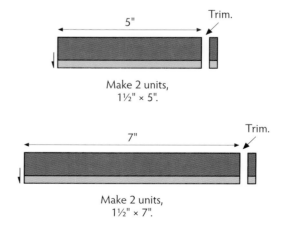

Make 2 units,
1½" × 5".

Make 2 units,
1½" × 7".

EXTRA SNIPPET

Twice-as-Nice Trimming

When trimming oversize units or strip sets to the specified size, I've learned to trim away a bit of excess length from *each* end, rather than just one end. This "trimming twice" approach leaves the more evenly stitched center area of the pieced unit for your needed patchwork, removing the portions where fishtailing is most likely to occur.

2. Join a 5" border unit to the right and left sides of the quilt center. Press the seam allowances away from the quilt center. Join a 7" border unit to each remaining side of the quilt center. Press the seam allowances away from the quilt center.

COMPLETING THE QUILT

Layer and baste the quilt top, batting, and backing. Quilt the layers. The featured quilt was hand quilted in the ditch (along the seam lines) of the blocks and border patchwork. The dark red portions of the border were stitched with a rope design running in one direction around the quilt. Join the teal binding strips to make one length and use it to bind the quilt.

Old Glory

Triangle patchwork meets stars, then more triangles, and then more stars—sometimes more actually is more! Gather prints in a rainbow of hues for a colorful approach, or personalize your palette and choose shades of red, cream, and blue for a more traditional Americana look.

MATERIALS

Yardages are based on a 42" usable width of fabric after prewashing and removing selvages. Refer to "Cutting Bias Strips" on page 119 to cut the bias strips. Please note that the featured quilt includes a mix of prints and plaids, but any blend of fabrics you choose will work beautifully.

+ 1 fat quarter (18" × 21") of cream check for flag stripes, flag star, and half-square-triangle units

+ 3 fat quarters of assorted cream prints for flag star, Star blocks, and half-square-triangle units

+ ⅜ yard of blue plaid for flag star, Star block, and binding

+ ¼ yard (not a fat quarter) of red plaid for flag stripes, Star block, and border

+ 6" × 6" square *each* of green, gold, orange, and brown plaid for Star blocks

+ 1 chubby sixteenth (9" × 10½") of teal plaid for Star block

+ 16 chubby sixteenths of assorted prints for half-square-triangle units

+ ⅔ yard of fabric for backing

+ 23" × 33" rectangle of batting

CUTTING

Cut all pieces across the width of the fabric in the order given unless otherwise noted.

From the cream check, cut:
2 strips, 2⅞" × 21"; crosscut into 8 squares, 2⅞" × 2⅞". Cut each square in half diagonally *once* to yield 2 triangles (total of 16).
1 strip, 1½" × 21"; crosscut into 8 squares, 1½" × 1½"
2 strips, 1" × 21"; crosscut into:
    2 rectangles, 1" × 8½"
    4 rectangles, 1" × 4½"
Reserve the remainder of the cream check for the Star blocks.

From the blue plaid, cut:
1 strip, 2½" × 42"; crosscut the strip into 1 square, 2½" × 2½". From the remainder of the strip, cut:
    4 rectangles, 1½" × 2½"
    12 squares, 1½" × 1½"
Enough 2½"-wide *bias* strips to make a 104" length of binding when joined end to end (for my chubby-binding method provided on page 127, reduce the strip width to 2")

From *each* of the 3 cream prints, cut:
2 strips, 2⅞" × 21"; crosscut into 8 squares, 2⅞" × 2⅞" (combined total of 24). Cut each square in half diagonally *once* to yield 2 triangles (combined total of 48).
2 strips, 1½" × 21"; crosscut into:
    8 rectangles, 1½" × 2½" (combined total of 24)
    8 squares, 1½" × 1½" (combined total of 24)
Reserve the remainder of the cream prints.

Continued on page 76

Continued from page 75

From the remainder of the reserved cream check and cream prints, cut a *total* of:

1 square, 2½" × 2½"

8 rectangles, 1½" × 2½"

8 squares, 1½" × 1½"

From the red plaid, cut;

3 strips, 1½" × 42"; crosscut into:

    2 strips, 1½" × 26½"

    2 strips, 1½" × 18½"

    8 squares, 1½" × 1½"

1 strip, 2½" × 42"; crosscut the strip into 1 square, 2½" × 2½". From the remainder of the strip, cut 2 rectangles, 1" × 8½", and 4 rectangles, 1" × 4½".

From *each* of the green, gold, orange, and brown plaid 6" squares, cut:

1 square, 2½" × 2½" (combined total of 4)

8 squares, 1½" × 1½" (combined total of 32)

Keep the squares organized in sets by color.

From the teal plaid, cut:

2 squares, 2½" × 2½"

16 squares, 1½" × 1½"

From *each* of the 16 assorted prints, cut:

2 squares, 2⅞" × 2⅞" (combined total of 32);

    cut each square in half diagonally *once* to yield

    2 triangles (combined total of 64)

PIECING THE FLAG UNIT

1. Select eight cream check 1½" squares, four blue plaid 1½" × 2½" rectangles, four blue plaid 1½" squares, and the cream print 2½" square. Use a pencil and an acrylic ruler to draw a diagonal sewing line from corner to corner on the wrong side of each cream check square.

2. Layer a prepared cream check square onto one end of a blue 1½" × 2½" rectangle. Stitch the pair together along the drawn line. Fold the resulting inner cream triangle open, aligning the corner with the corner of the blue rectangle. Press. Trim away the layers beneath the top triangle, leaving a ¼" seam allowance. In the same manner, add a mirror-image triangle to the remaining end of the blue rectangle. Repeat to piece a total of four star-point units measuring 1½" × 2½", including the seam allowances.

Make 4 star-point units,
1½" × 2½".

Old Glory

FINISHED QUILT SIZE: 18½" × 28½" ✦ FINISHED BLOCK SIZE: 4" × 4"

Designed and pieced by Kim Diehl. Machine quilted by Rebecca Silbaugh.

3. Lay out the four star-point units, the four blue 1½" squares, and the cream print 2½" square in three horizontal rows. Join the pieces in each row. Press. Join the rows. Press. The pieced Star block should measure 4½" square, including the seam allowances.

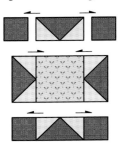
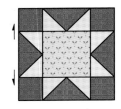

Star block,
4½" × 4½"

4. Lay out four red plaid and four cream check 1" × 4½" rectangles in alternating positions. Join the rectangles along the long edges. Press. Join this pieced unit to the Star block. The partial flag unit should now measure 4½" × 8½", including the seam allowances.

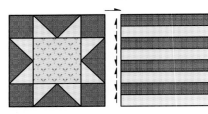

Partial flag unit,
4½" × 8½"

5. Lay out and join two red plaid and two cream check 1" × 8½" rectangles in alternating positions. Press the seam allowances toward the red rectangles. Join this pieced unit to the bottom of the partial flag unit. Press. The pieced flag unit should measure 6½" × 8½", including the seam allowances.

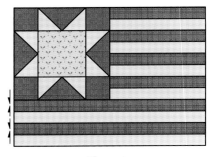

Flag unit,
6½" × 8½"

PIECING THE STAR BLOCKS

1. Select the pieces cut from the blue, green, gold, orange, brown, and teal plaid, and the remainder of the red plaid pieces. Draw a diagonal sewing line on each of the 1½" squares as previously instructed.

2. Using one plaid 2½" square, eight prepared matching plaid 1½" squares, four assorted cream 1½" × 2½" rectangles, and four assorted cream 1½" squares for each star, repeat steps 2 and 3 of "Piecing the Flag Unit" beginning on page 76 to piece a Star block measuring 4½" square, including the seam allowances. Repeat to piece a total of eight Star blocks.

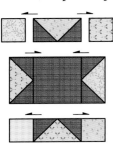
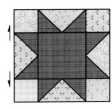

Make 8 Star blocks,
4½" × 4½".

PIECING THE TRIANGLE ROWS

1. Choosing the prints randomly, join a print and a cream 2⅞" triangle along the long diagonal edges. Press. Trim away the dog-ear points. Repeat to piece a total of 64 half-square-triangle units measuring 2½" square, including the seam allowances.

Make 64 units,
2½" × 2½".

2. Join two half-square-triangle units as shown. Press. Repeat to piece a total of six short triangle rows measuring 2½" × 4½", including the seam allowances.

Make 6 short triangle rows,
2½" × 4½".

Old Glory

3. Join eight half-square-triangle units end to end. Press. Repeat to piece a total of six long triangle rows measuring 2½" × 16½", including the seam allowances. Please note that you'll have four unused half-square-triangle units; these have been included for added choices as you stitch the patchwork.

Make 6 long triangle rows,
2½" × 16½".

PIECING THE QUILT CENTER

1. Join three short triangle rows along the long edges. Press. Repeat to piece side triangle units. Referring to the illustration at right, join these units to the right and left sides of the flag unit. Press. The flag patchwork unit should measure 6½" × 16½", including the seam allowances.

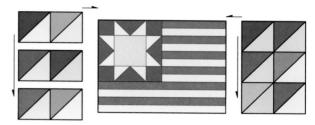

Flag unit,
6½" × 16½"

2. Referring to the quilt assembly diagram on page 80, join two long triangle rows to the top of the flag unit. Press. In the same manner, join two long triangle rows to the bottom of the flag unit. Press.

EXTRA SNIPPET

Displaying Little Quilts

For a unique way to display your small quilts, try folding and stacking them onto a vintage child-sized chair. These little chairs are easy to find in secondhand stores and antique shops, and depending upon the style, they can be placed on a tabletop or even hung on the wall. Mix and mingle several quilts for everyday charm, or group them by theme or color as the seasons and holidays change. The possibilities are endless!

3. Choosing the colors randomly, join four pieced Star blocks end to end. Press. Repeat to piece a total of two star rows measuring 4½" × 16½", including the seam allowances. Join one star row to the top edge of the patchwork unit and one star row to the bottom edge of the patchwork unit. Press.

4. Join one long triangle row to the top of the patchwork unit and the remaining long triangle row to the bottom of the patchwork unit. Press. The pieced quilt center should now measure 16½" × 26½", including the seam allowances.

Quilt assembly

ADDING THE BORDER

Join a red plaid 1½" × 26½" strip to the right and left sides of the quilt center. Press the seam allowances toward the red strips. Join a red plaid 1½" × 18½" strip to the top and bottom of the quilt center. Press the seam allowances toward the red strips.

EXTRA SNIPPET

Brilliant Binding

When I'm doubtful about the best binding choice for a given scrappy quilt, I choose a print used near the quilt center. This trick gives the quilt a cohesive feel, because the print acts as a "bridge" between the center and the outer bound edges.

COMPLETING THE QUILT

Layer and baste the quilt top, batting, and backing. Quilt the layers. The Star blocks of the featured quilt were machine quilted with diagonal lines to form a secondary star shape, and the perimeter of each block was stitched in the ditch (along the seam lines). The diagonal triangle seams were also stitched in the ditch, with an apple-core design included on each triangle unit in the quilt center. The top and bottom triangle rows were stitched with repeating diagonal lines, and this pattern was duplicated on the flag stripes. Last, the border was stitched with a continuous string of circles. Join the blue plaid bias strips to make one length and use it to bind the quilt.

Prairie Sky

Look closely at this mini-quilt and you'll discover that it offers more than one perspective. Glance from one direction and you may be treated to a sprinkling of creamy stars, but change your focus and you'll see richly hued stars drifting among the clouds. It's all about your point of view!

MATERIALS

- 1 fat quarter (18" × 21") of dark print for patchwork and binding
- 23 charm squares (5" × 5") of assorted prints for patchwork
- 4 fat eighths (9" × 21") of assorted cream prints for diamond appliqués
- 1 fat quarter of fabric for backing
- 15" × 17" rectangle of batting
- Fabric glue stick*
- Liquid glue for fabric, water-soluble and acid-free*
- Freezer paper*
- .004 monofilament thread*

These supplies will enable you to use my invisible machine-appliqué method, or you can substitute your own favorite appliqué technique.

CUTTING

Cut all pieces across the width of the fabric in the order given unless otherwise noted. For greater ease, cutting instructions for the appliqués are provided separately.

From the dark print, cut:
3 binding strips, 2½" × 21" (for my chubby-binding method provided on page 127, reduce the strip width to 2")
Reserve the remainder of the dark print.

From the 23 assorted prints and the reserved remainder of the dark print, cut a combined total of:
20 squares, 2½" × 2½"
18 rectangles, 1½" × 2½"
4 squares, 1½" × 1½"

PIECING THE QUILT CENTER

Sew all pieces with right sides together using a ¼" seam allowance. Press the seam allowances as indicated by the arrows or otherwise specified.

1. With right sides together, fold one of the print 2½" squares in half and use a hot, dry iron to lightly press the horizontal center crease. Unfold and refold the square to press a vertical center crease. Repeat to prepare a total of 20 assorted print 2½" squares.

Prepare 20 squares, 2½" × 2½".

2. Join four prepared assorted print 2½" squares end to end. Carefully press, using caution not to remove the pressed creases. Repeat to piece a total of five rows, 2½" × 8½", including the seam allowances.

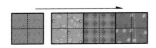

Make 5 rows,
2½" × 8½".

3. Lay out the rows, turning every other row so that the seams are resting in opposite directions and will nest together. Join the rows. Press the seam allowances toward the bottom of the unit. The pieced quilt center should measure 8½" × 10½", including the seam allowances.

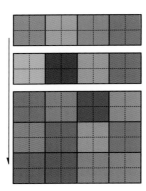

Quilt center,
8½" × 10½"

Preparing and Stitching the Diamond Appliqués

The steps outlined below incorporate my invisible machine-appliqué method (see page 121), because it makes stitching the appliqués in this project a snap. If preferred, substitute your own favorite method. Full-diamond and half-diamond appliqué patterns are provided on page 87.

1. Referring to "Preparing Pattern-Tracing Templates" on page 121, use freezer paper to prepare a full-diamond and half-diamond pattern-tracing template. Cut and stack five to six pieces of freezer paper, all dull side up. Use the prepared full-diamond template and a pencil to trace the shape onto the top sheet of paper. Anchor the layers together through the center of the diamond using a straight pin. Use a rotary cutter and an acrylic ruler to cut the diamond pattern pieces from the layered stack, cutting exactly on the drawn lines. Repeat to prepare a total of 31 full-diamond pattern pieces and 18 half-diamond pattern pieces.

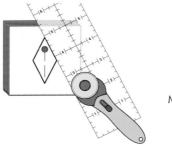

Make 31.   Make 18.

2. Apply a small dab of fabric glue stick to the center of the nonwaxy, dull side of a full-diamond pattern piece and affix it shiny side up to the *wrong* side of one of the cream prints. Use a rotary cutter and an acrylic ruler to cut out the shape, adding a ¼" seam allowance on all sides. Repeat using the remaining pattern pieces to cut a total of 31 full-diamond and 18 half-diamond appliqués from the four cream prints.

Make 31.   Make 18.

EXTRA SNIPPET

Reducing Bulk

When working with appliqués that have angles such as those at the top and bottom points of the diamond shape in this project, the ¼" seam allowance can sometimes add bulk and make it slightly challenging to turn under the edges for stitching. Experience has taught me that trimming away the excess fabric at these narrow points a scant ¼" out from the paper pattern piece will remove much of the excess bulk and simplify the preparation steps.

3. Starting on one side (not a point) of a prepared full diamond, use a hot, dry iron to work in a counterclockwise direction around the shape and press the seam allowance onto the waxy side of the pattern piece. Apply a small amount of fabric glue stick to the fabric seam allowance at each point. Use an awl to grab and sweep the glued cloth onto the wrong side of the piece; use the hot iron to anchor each point in place. Repeat to prepare all full-diamond and half-diamond appliqués for stitching. Don't press under the raw edges of the flat top edges of the half-diamonds.

Leave the straight edge unpressed.

4. Using the quilt pictured on page 86 as a guide, use the pressed creases on each patchwork square to center and position a prepared full-diamond appliqué. When you're pleased with the arrangement of diamond prints, apply small dots of liquid fabric glue to the fabric seam allowance on the wrong side of each appliqué and reposition it. Heat set the appliqués with a hot iron from the back of the unit. In the same manner, position, glue baste, and heat set the half-diamond appliqués around the outer edge of the unit.

5. Referring to "Stitching the Appliqués" on page 124, or substituting your own favorite method, appliqué the shapes in place. From the back of the unit, carefully cut away the fabric underneath each appliqué, leaving a ¼" seam allowance, and remove the paper pattern pieces.

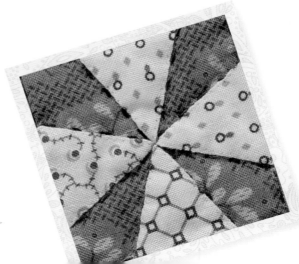

Prairie Sky

PIECING AND ADDING THE BORDER

1. Referring to the quilt assembly diagram, join five assorted print 1½" × 2½" rectangles end to end. Press. Repeat to piece a total of two long border strips measuring 1½" × 10½", including the seam allowances. In the same manner, using four assorted print 1½" × 2½" rectangles per strip, piece two short border strips measuring 1½" × 8½", including the seam allowances.

2. Join a long border strip to the right and left sides of the quilt center. Press. Join a print 1½" square to each end of the short border strips. Press. Join these strips to the top and bottom edges of the quilt center. Press.

COMPLETING THE QUILT

Layer and baste the quilt top, batting, and backing. Quilt the layers. The featured project was hand quilted in the big-stitch method as described in "Big-Stitch Hand Quilting" on page 126. The diamond appliqués in the quilt center were outlined and the patchwork was stitched in the ditch (along the seam lines). Xs were quilted onto the border rectangles and squares. Join the dark binding strips to make one length and use it to bind the quilt.

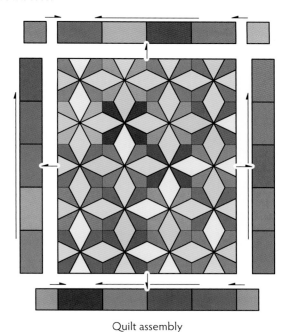

Quilt assembly

Patterns do not include seam allowances.

Half-diamond

Straight of grain

Full Diamond

Matchsticks

If you like saving the most ridiculously small snippets of your favorite prints because you can't bring yourself to toss them, you're just like me! The "matchstick" pieces in this small quilt are perfect for rescuing treasured pieces and giving them one last chance to be fabulous.

MATERIALS

Yardages are based on a 42" usable width of fabric after prewashing and removing selvages.

- 1 fat eighth (9" × 21") of brown print for patchwork and border
- 1 fat quarter (18" × 21") of teal print for patchwork and binding
- Approximately ⅜ yard *total* of assorted dark print scraps for patchwork
- Approximately ⅜ yard *total* of assorted cream print scraps for patchwork
- ⅝ yard of fabric for backing
- 21" × 22" rectangle of batting

CUTTING

Cut all pieces across the width of the fabric in the order given unless otherwise noted. For added choices as you piece the blocks, you may wish to cut a handful of extra pieces in each given size from the assorted dark and cream prints.

From the brown print, cut:
2 strips, 1½" × 15½"
2 strips, 1½" × 17"
Reserve the remainder of the brown print.

From the teal print, cut:
4 binding strips, 2½" × 21" (for my chubby-binding method provided on page 127, reduce the strip width to 2")
Reserve the remainder of the teal print.

From the assorted dark print scraps and the reserved remainder of the brown and teal prints, cut a *combined total* of:
36 squares, 1" × 1"
36 rectangles, 1" × 1½"
36 rectangles, 1" × 2"
36 rectangles, 1" × 2½"
15 rectangles, 1" × 3"

From the assorted cream print scraps, cut a *combined total* of:
36 squares, 1" × 1"
36 rectangles, 1" × 1½"
36 rectangles, 1" × 2"
36 rectangles, 1" × 2½"
15 rectangles, 1" × 3"

PIECING THE
MATCHSTICK BLOCKS

Sew all pieces with right sides together using a ¼" seam allowance. Press the seam allowances as indicated by the arrows or otherwise specified.

1. Join a dark 1" square to a cream 1" × 2½" rectangle. Press. Repeat to piece a total of 36 A units measuring 1" × 3", including the seam allowances.

Make 36 A units,
1" × 3".

2. Continue joining dark and cream squares and rectangles as shown to piece 36 each of the B, C, and D units. Each unit should measure 1" × 3", including the seam allowances.

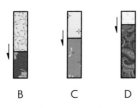

B   C   D

Make 36 of each unit,
1" × 3".

3. Lay out one each of the A, B, C, and D units. Join the units. Press. Repeat to piece a total of 18 Matchstick blocks measuring 2½" × 3", including the seam allowances.

A B C D

Make 18 Matchstick blocks,
2½" × 3".

4. Repeat step 3 to piece a total of 18 mirror-image Matchstick blocks measuring 2½" × 3", including the seam allowances.

D C B A

Make 18 mirror-image
Matchstick blocks,
2½" × 3".

Matchsticks

Designed and pieced by Kim Diehl. Machine quilted by Connie Tabor.

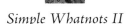
5. Lay out three Matchstick blocks, three mirror-image Matchstick blocks, three dark 1" × 3" setting rectangles, and two cream 1" × 3" setting rectangles as shown. Join the pieces. Press. Repeat to piece a total of three upper strips, 3" × 15", including the seam allowances.

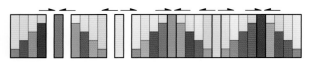

Make 3 upper strips,
3" × 15".

6. Again referring to the illustration, lay out three mirror-image Matchstick blocks, three Matchstick blocks, three cream 1" × 3" setting rectangles, and two dark 1" × 3" setting rectangles. Join the pieces. Press. Repeat to piece a total of three lower strips, 3" × 15", including the seam allowances.

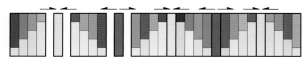

Make 3 lower strips,
3" × 15".

7. Join an upper strip from step 5 to a lower strip from step 6. Press. Repeat to piece a total of three block rows measuring 5½" × 15", including the seam allowances.

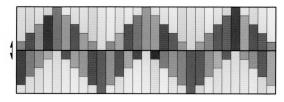

Make 3 block rows,
5½" × 15".

8. Referring to the quilt pictured on page 91, lay out the three block rows. Join the rows. Press the seam allowances open. The pieced quilt center should measure 15" × 15½", including the seam allowances.

Referring to the quilt pictured on page 91

EXTRA SNIPPET

Versatility!

Like so many pieced blocks featuring strips, the Matchstick blocks in this project can be set in a variety of ways to produce endless design alternatives. With a simple and quick shuffle of the blocks, they can be mixed, mingled, turned, and rearranged to create surprising and unexpected patterns. I hope you'll embrace these scrappy patchwork blocks and explore the many possibilities they bring.

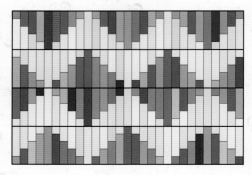

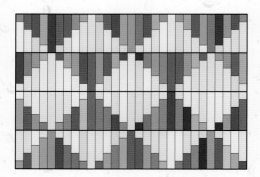

Adding the Border

Join a brown 1½" × 15½" strip to the right and left sides of the quilt center. Press the seam allowances toward the border. Join a brown 1½" × 17" strip to each remaining side of the quilt center. Press the seam allowances toward the border.

Completing the Quilt

Layer and baste the quilt top, batting, and backing. Quilt the layers. The featured quilt was machine quilted with an edge-to-edge design resembling chicken wire. Join the teal binding strips to make one length and use it to bind the quilt.

Idaho Lily

With its classic red and green color scheme, this compelling quilt is ideal for adding year-round charm to your home. Pair it with scented garden bouquets during warm-weather months, and when the snow flies, swap your garden glories for a bowl of fresh and fragrant evergreens.

MATERIALS

Yardage is based on a 42" usable width of fabric after prewashing and removing selvages.

+ ¾ yard of red floral for block patchwork, middle border, outer border, and binding
+ 5 chubby sixteenths (9" × 10½") of assorted red prints for block patchwork and middle border
+ ½ yard of cream print A for block patchwork, sashing, and inner border
+ 1 fat quarter (18" × 21") of cream print B for middle border
+ 1 chubby sixteenth of green print A for block patchwork, leaf appliqués, and middle border
+ 1 chubby sixteenth of green print B for stems and middle border
+ 1 chubby sixteenth of green print C for leaf appliqués, middle border, and outer border
+ 3 chubby sixteenths of assorted green prints for leaf appliqués and middle border
+ 1 yard of fabric for backing
+ 32" × 32" square of batting
+ Bias bar to make ⅜"-wide stems
+ Supplies for your favorite appliqué method
+ Liquid glue for fabric, water-soluble and acid-free
+ Fabric glue stick

CUTTING

Cut all pieces across the width of the fabric in the order given unless otherwise noted. Refer to "Cutting Bias Strips" on page 119 to cut bias strips. For greater ease, cutting instructions for the leaf appliqués are provided separately.

From the red floral, cut:
3 binding strips, 2½" × 42" (for my chubby binding method provided on page 127, reduce the strip width to 2")
4 strips, 3½" × 42"; crosscut into 4 strips, 3½" × 21½". From the remainder of these strips, cut:
    2 squares, 2½" × 2½"
    8 squares, 1½" × 1½"
The squares cut will make a total of 2 sets of squares for lilies. Reserve the remainder of the red floral.

Continued on page 96

Continued from page 95

From the assorted red prints, cut a *total* of 14 sets of:
1 square, 2½" × 2½" (combined total of 14)
4 squares, 1½" × 1½" (combined total of 56)
With the 2 red floral sets previously cut, you'll have a
combined total of 16 sets of squares for lilies. Keep
each of the red sets organized by print. Reserve the
remainder of the assorted red prints.

From the reserved remainder of all red prints, cut:
19 squares, 1⅞" × 1⅞"; cut each square in half diagonally
once to yield 2 triangles (combined total of 38)

From cream print A, cut:
2 strips, 2½" × 42"; crosscut into:
    4 rectangles, 2½" × 8½"
    8 rectangles, 2½" × 3½"
6 strips, 1½" × 42"; crosscut into:
    2 strips, 1½" × 19½"
    3 strips, 1½" × 17½"
    2 rectangles, 1½" × 8½"
    32 rectangles, 1½" × 2½"
    16 squares, 1½" × 1½"

From cream print B, cut:
4 strips, 1⅞" × 21"; crosscut into 38 squares,
    1⅞" × 1⅞". Cut each square in half diagonally *once*
    to yield 2 triangles (combined total of 76).
4 squares, 1½" × 1½"

From green print A, cut:
16 squares, 1½" × 1½"
Reserve the remainder of green print A.

From green print B, cut:
8 *bias* strips, 1¼" × 4"
Reserve the remainder of green print B.

From green print C, cut:
4 squares, 3½" × 3½"
Reserve the remainder of green print C.

**From the reserved remainder of all green prints and
the remaining green chubby sixteenths, cut a
combined total of:**
19 squares, 1⅞" × 1⅞"; cut each square in half diagonally
    once to yield 2 triangles (combined total of 38)
Reserve the scraps of all green prints for the leaf
    appliqués.

PIECING THE BLOCKS

*Sew all pieces with right sides together using a ¼" seam
allowance. Press the seam allowances as indicated by
the arrows.*

1. Use a pencil and an acrylic ruler to draw a diagonal
sewing line from corner to corner on the wrong side of
each red 1½" square. Return the prepared squares to
their original sets and continue to keep them organized
by print. In the same manner, draw a diagonal sewing
line on the wrong side of each green A 1½" square.

2. Select a set of red patchwork pieces. Layer a
prepared green print square onto one corner of the red
2½" square. Stitch the pair together along the drawn
diagonal line. Fold the resulting inner triangle open,
aligning the corner with the corner of the red square.
Press. Trim away the layers beneath the top triangle,
leaving a ¼" seam allowance. Repeat for a total of 16
flower-base units measuring 2½" square, including the
seam allowances.

Make 16 units,
2½" × 2½".

3. Layer a prepared red square onto one end of a
cream A 1½" × 2½" rectangle. Stitch, press, and trim
as previously instructed. In the same manner, stitch
a mirror-image point onto the remaining corner of
the rectangle using a matching prepared red square.
Repeat for a total of 32 flying-geese units measuring
1½" × 2½", including the seam allowances.

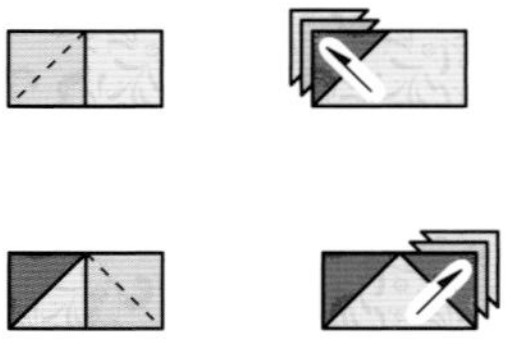

Make 32 units,
1½" × 2½".

4. Using units from steps 2 and 3 made with a single red print, lay out one flower-base unit, two flying-geese units, and one cream A 1½" square in two horizontal rows. Join the pieces in each row. Press. Join the rows. Press. Repeat for a total of 16 flower units measuring 3½" square, including the seam allowances.

5. Lay out four pieced flower units, two cream A 2½" × 3½" rectangles, and one cream A 2½" × 8½" rectangle in three horizontal rows. Join the pieces in the top and bottom rows. Press. Join the rows. Press. Repeat for a total of four pieced blocks measuring 8½" square, including the seam allowances.

Make 16 units, 3½" × 3½".

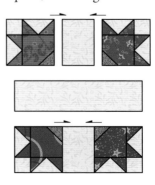

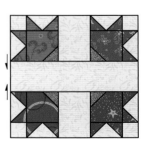

Make 4 blocks, 8½" × 8½".

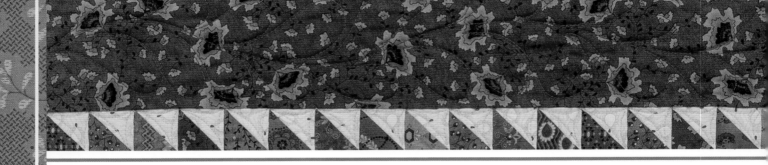

APPLIQUÉING THE BLOCKS

Step-by-step instructions for my invisible machine-appliqué method begin on page 121, or you can substitute your own favorite method. The leaf appliqué pattern is provided on page 101.

1. Referring to "Making Bias-Tube Stems and Vines" on page 123, prepare the stems using the green B bias strips. Apply fabric glue stick to each wrong-side end of the stems. Fold the ends under, sizing the folds so that the stems will overlap approximately ¼" onto the flower base when positioned diagonally on the block centers. Use a hot, dry iron to heat set the ends and anchor them in place.

2. Apply dots of liquid glue to the seam allowance of two prepared stems at approximately ½" intervals. Position the glue-basted stems onto a block. From the back of the block, use a hot, dry iron to heat set the stems. Repeat for all four blocks.

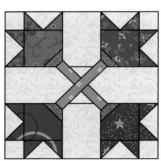

Make 4.

3. From the scraps of all green prints, excluding the stem print, cut and prepare 16 leaves.

4. Using the quilt pictured on page 99 as a guide, position a prepared leaf in each space between the intersecting stems. Use your favorite appliqué method to stitch the stems and leaves in place. Repeat for a total of four appliquéd blocks.

PIECING THE QUILT CENTER

Referring to the quilt assembly diagram below, lay out the four blocks, two cream A 1½" × 8½" rectangles, and one cream A 1½" × 17½" strip in three rows to form the quilt center. Join the pieces in the top and bottom rows. Press. Join the rows. Press. The pieced quilt center should measure 17½" square, including the seam allowances.

Quilt assembly

ADDING THE INNER BORDER

Join a cream A 1½" × 17½" strip to the right and left sides of the pieced quilt center. Press the seam allowances toward the strips. Join a cream A 1½" × 19½" strip to the remaining sides of the quilt center. Press the seam allowances toward the strips. The quilt top should now measure 19½" square, including the seam allowances.

Idaho Lily

FINISHED QUILT SIZE: 27½" × 27½" • FINISHED BLOCK SIZE: 8" × 8"

Designed and pieced by Kim Diehl. Machine quilted by Deborah Poole.

PIECING AND ADDING THE MIDDLE BORDER

1. Join a cream B and a red 1⅞" triangle along the long diagonal edges. Press. Trim away the dog-ear points. Repeat for a total of 38 red half-square-triangle units measuring 1½" × 1½", including the seam allowances. In the same manner, join the cream B and green 1⅞" triangles to make 38 green half-square-triangle units.

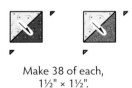

Make 38 of each,
1½" × 1½".

2. Lay out a total of 19 red and green half-square-triangle units end to end in random order but all facing in the same direction. Join the units. Press. Repeat for a total of four pieced middle-border strips measuring 1½" × 19½", including the seam allowances. (**Note:** Whoops! I incorrectly calculated the number of half-square-triangle units when I made the sample in

the photo on page 99. Rest assured that 19 is the mathematically correct number.)

Make 4 middle-border strips,
1½" × 19½".

3. Referring to the pictured quilt, join a pieced middle-border strip to the right and left sides of the quilt top. Press the seam allowances toward the quilt center. Join a cream B 1½" square to each end of the remaining pieced middle-border strips. Press the seam allowances toward the cream squares. Join these pieced strips to the remaining sides of the quilt top. Press the seam allowances toward the quilt center.

ADDING THE OUTER BORDER

Join a red floral 3½" × 21½" strip to the right and left sides of the quilt top. Press the seam allowances toward the red strips. Join a green C 3½" square to each end of the remaining red floral strips. Press the seam allowances toward the strips. Join the strips to the top and bottom of the quilt top. Press the seam allowances toward the red strips.

COMPLETING THE QUILT

Layer the quilt top, batting, and backing. Quilt the layers. The featured quilt was machine quilted with a small-scale swirling design stitched onto the cream background, and free-form intersecting lines were stitched onto the red flowers to resemble veining. Curved lines were stitched on each side of the half-square-triangle center seams. A serpentine feathered design was quilted onto the outer border, and Xs were stitched onto the middle- and outer-border corner squares. Join the red floral binding strips to make one length and use it to bind the quilt.

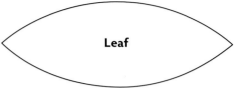

Leaf

Pattern does not include seam allowance.

EXTRA SNIPPET

Triangle Tricks

With a few simple tricks, triangle patchwork can be easy to stitch . . . honest! Here's a quick overview of the steps I use:

- When layering triangles for stitching, I always align the corners, *not* the long diagonal edges. This approach enables any size differences to be absorbed into the seam allowance.

- Next, I use a *scant* ¼" seam allowance to stitch the layered diagonal edges, producing a slightly oversized pieced unit.

- Here's where the magic happens. Instead of trimming away the dog-ear points with scissors, I use a square acrylic ruler with a marked center diagonal line to trim the unit to the proper size and remove the dog-ear points all in the same step. Place the unit on a cutting mat and center the ruler onto it with the diagonal line positioned over the diagonal seam. Use a rotary cutter to remove any excess fabric on the side and top edges. Then, rotate the unit and reposition the ruler, aligning the previously trimmed fabric edges with the appropriate ruler measurement, and trim the remaining sides.

Using these quick steps *now* will save a ton of time *later*, because the accurately sized units will fit together precisely as the remainder of the project is stitched.

Henpecked

A sweet little patchwork project, with its myriad of scrappy half-square-triangle blocks, is just right for raiding your scrap basket for those last bits of favorite fabrics. Choose small-scale prints in a rainbow of colors, finish with a dollop of big-stitch hand quilting, and you're done!

MATERIALS

- 4 chubby sixteenths (9" × 10½") of assorted tan prints for blocks
- 23 charm squares (5" × 5") of assorted prints for blocks
- 1 fat quarter (18" × 21") of brown print for blocks and binding
- 12 strips, 2" × 12", of assorted prints for Log Cabin border
- 1 fat quarter of fabric for backing
- 15" × 16" rectangle of batting

CUTTING

Cut all pieces across the width of the fabric in the order given unless otherwise noted.

From *each* of the assorted tan prints, cut:
5 squares, 1⅞" × 1⅞" (combined total of 20); cut each square in half diagonally *once* to yield 2 triangles (combined total of 40)

From the brown print, cut:
3 binding strips, 2½" × 21" (for my chubby-binding method provided on page 127, reduce the strip width to 2")
Reserve the remainder of the brown print.

From *each* of the 23 assorted print charm squares and the reserved remainder of the brown print, cut:
1 square, 1⅞" × 1⅞" (combined total of 24); cut each square in half diagonally *once* to yield 2 triangles (combined total of 48)

From the 12 assorted print strips for the Log Cabin border, cut a *combined total* of:
2 strips, 1½" × 10½"
2 strips, 1½" × 8½"
2 strips, 1½" × 7½"
2 strips, 1" × 10½"
2 strips, 1" × 8½"
2 strips, 1" × 7½"

Patchwork Perfection

Don't be intimidated by the small-scale patchwork featured in this project—with the right approach, accuracy can be easy to achieve! Here's a quick summary of the simple steps I use, especially when stitching petite projects.

- Reduce your stitch length to make it slightly shorter than your usual length. For my sewing machine, I reduce the stitch length from 2.2 to 1.8 to help my sewn seams remain secure from edge to edge.

- Because we all feed patchwork through our sewing machines differently, using a ¼" presser foot won't necessarily guarantee an accurate ¼" seam allowance. Before beginning a small project, I've learned to take a moment to check the accuracy of my seams. To do this, cut three rectangles, 1½" × 3", from scraps. Piece the rectangles together along the long edges and press the seam allowances away from the center rectangle. The width of the center rectangle should measure 1". If the width is too narrow, rest your patchwork a bit more softly against the ¼" foot as you stitch future units. For a rectangle that's too wide, rest your patchwork a bit more firmly against the edge of the ¼" foot.

It's well worth the small amount of time it takes to incorporate these simple steps into your sewing routine!

PIECING THE HALF-SQUARE TRIANGLE BLOCKS

Sew all pieces with right sides together using a ¼" seam allowance. Press the seam allowances as indicated by the arrows.

Join an assorted print and a tan 1⅞" triangle along the long diagonal edges. Press. Trim away the dog-ear points. Repeat for a total of 40 pieced Half-Square-Triangle blocks measuring 1½" square, including the seam allowances. Please note that you'll have eight unused assorted print triangles; these have been included for added versatility as you stitch your patchwork.

Make 40 blocks,
1½" × 1½".

PIECING THE QUILT CENTER

1. Using the quilt pictured on page 102 as a guide, lay out five pieced Half-Square-Triangle blocks. Join the blocks. Press. Repeat for a total of four rows, 1½" × 5½", for rows 1, 3, 5, and 7.

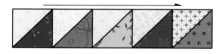

Make 4 odd-numbered rows,
1½" × 5½".

2. Repeat step 1 to make rows 2, 4, and 6. Press the seam allowances in the opposite direction so they'll nest together. You'll have five unused Half-Square-Triangle blocks; these have been included for added versatility as you piece the quilt-center rows.

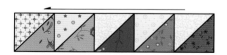

Make 3 even-numbered rows,
1½" × 5½".

3. Referring to the quilt-assembly diagram, lay out the pieced rows, alternating the odd- and even-numbered rows so that the pressed seam allowances will nest together when they're joined. Join the rows. Press the seam allowances open. The pieced quilt center should measure 5½" × 7½", including the seam allowances.

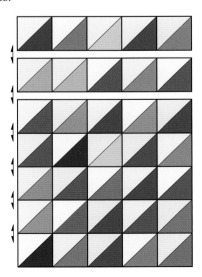

Quilt assembly

Finished quilt size: 10½" × 11½" ✦ **Finished block size:** 1" × 1"

Designed, pieced, and hand quilted in the big-stitch method by Kim Diehl.

ADDING THE LOG CABIN BORDER

Referring to the adding the borders illustration and beginning with the 1½" × 7½" strips, join a strip to the right and left sides of the quilt center. Continue joining and pressing strips as indicated to build the border.

COMPLETING THE QUILT

Layer the quilt top, batting, and backing. Quilt the layers. The featured quilt was hand quilted in the big-stitch method as described in "Big-Stitch Hand Quilting" on page 126. The blocks were stitched in the ditch (along the seam lines), and curved lines were quilted onto the tan portion of each Half-Square-Triangle block along the diagonal seam. The narrow Log Cabin border strips were stitched in the ditch, and a straight line was stitched through the center of each wide Log Cabin strip. Join the brown binding strips to make one length and use it to bind the quilt.

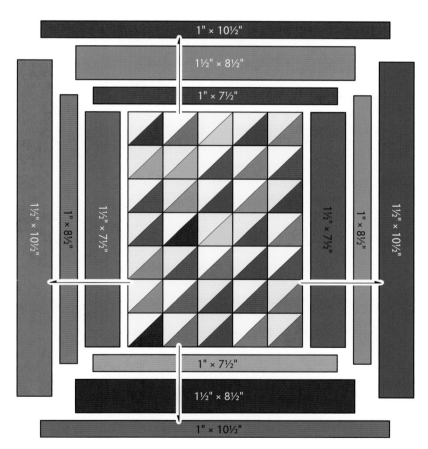

Adding the borders

Linen Drawer

Simple squares and rectangles look anything but simple when thoughtfully arranged and stitched into a repeating pattern of "woven" pieces. Choosing an array of colorful prints gives this quilt an effervescent look, a bit like fairy dust straight from the sewing room!

FINISHED TABLE-RUNNER SIZE: 13½" × 25½"

Designed and pieced by Kim Diehl.

Machine quilted by Connie Tabor.

MATERIALS

Yardage is based on a 42" usable width of fabric after prewashing and removing selvages.

- Approximately ⅔ yard *total* of assorted print scraps for patchwork
- 1 fat quarter (18" × 21") of complementary print for patchwork and binding
- ⅝ yard of fabric for backing
- 18" × 30" rectangle of batting

CUTTING

Cut all pieces across the width of the fabric in the order given unless otherwise noted.

From the fat quarter of complementary print, cut:
5 binding strips, 2½" × 21" (for my chubby-binding method provided on page 127, reduce the strip width to 2")
Reserve the remainder of the complementary print.

From the assorted print scraps and the reserved remainder of the complementary print, cut a combined total of:
108 rectangles, 1½" × 2½"
45 squares, 1½" × 1½"
16 squares, 2½" × 2½"

page 127

EXTRA SNIPPET

Successfully Scrappy

The simple squares and rectangles featured in this table runner make it an ideal scrap buster, and choosing a good blend of dark, medium, *and* light prints will help it sparkle. To achieve a sense of balance without any single patchwork unit becoming a bull's-eye, I primarily chose to use my lightest and brightest prints for the smaller pieces.

Another secret to successfully incorporating a print that's a bit different from the others is to use it twice or more, spacing it at intervals across the quilt top. Using a print with a different look only once can cause it to stand out and seem like an accident, while using it twice or more provides balance, makes your choice look intentional, and adds a bit of magic to your color scheme.

PIECING THE PATCHWORK ROWS

Sew all pieces with right sides together using a ¼" seam allowance. Press the seam allowances as indicated by the arrows or otherwise specified.

1. Join two assorted print 1½" × 2½" rectangles along the long edges. Press. Repeat to piece a total of 16 patchwork squares measuring 2½" square, including the seam allowances.

Make 16 units,
2½" × 2½".

2. Lay out five 1½" squares and four 1½" × 2½" rectangles in alternating positions. Join the pieces. Press. Repeat to piece a total of nine A rows measuring 1½" × 13½", including the seam allowances.

Make 9 A rows,
1½" × 13½".

3. Lay out five 1½" × 2½" rectangles, two 2½" squares, and two units from step 1 as shown. Join the pieces. Press. Repeat to piece a total of four B rows measuring 2½" × 13½", including the seam allowances.

Make 4 B rows,
2½" × 13½".

4. Lay out five 1½" × 2½" rectangles, two units from step 1, and two 2½" squares as shown. Join the pieces. Press. Repeat to piece a total of four C rows measuring 2½" × 13½", including the seam allowances.

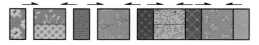

Make 4 C rows,
2½" × 13½".

PIECING THE TABLE RUNNER

Referring to the table-runner assembly diagram, lay out the patchwork A, B, and C rows. Join the rows. Press.

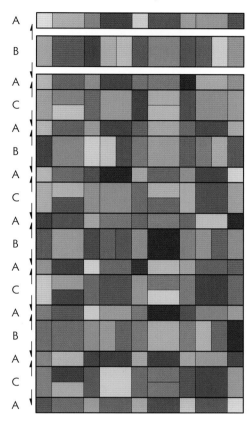

Quilt assembly

COMPLETING THE TABLE RUNNER

Layer and baste the table-runner top, batting, and backing. Quilt the layers. The featured table runner was quilted with an edge-to-edge echoed orange-peel design to provide balance and soften the many straight lines featured in the patchwork. Join the complementary print binding strips to make one length and use it to bind the runner.

EXTRA SNIPPET

Endless Options

Once the pattern of rectangles and squares has been established, it's super easy to personalize this patchwork project to suit your needs: simply add or subtract rows, pieced units, rectangles, and/or squares to achieve your goal. You can transform this runner and size it up to be an amazingly colorful scrap-busting lap quilt, size it down to fit the smallest tabletop niche, keep it rectangular, or make it square. The design is fun to stitch, produces quick results, and, because of its versatility, brings endless options to the table.

Tussie-Mussie

Thoughtfully placed colors and easily enhanced patchwork points transform star blocks into star blossoms! Embellish your handiwork with turn-free appliqué stems and a scattering of gently shaped leaves, and your indoor bouquet will be in bloom for many seasons to come.

MATERIALS

* 1 fat eighth (9" × 21") of cream print for Starflower block and flying-geese border
* 6 charm squares (5" × 5") of assorted red prints for Starflower block and flying-geese border
* 1 chubby sixteenth (9" × 10½") of dark red print for Starflower block and flying-geese border
* 6 charm squares of assorted aqua, turquoise, and teal prints (collectively referred to as "aqua") for Starflower block and checkerboard border
* 1 fat quarter (18" × 21") of dark teal print for Starflower block, checkerboard border, and binding
* 1 fat eighth of medium red check for inner border
* 1 fat quarter of fabric for backing
* 15" × 19" rectangle of batting
* Bias bar to make ⅜"-wide stems
* Freezer paper
* Fabric glue stick
* Liquid glue for fabric, water-soluble and acid-free
* Supplies for your favorite appliqué method

CUTTING

Cut all pieces across the width of the fabric in the order given unless otherwise noted. Refer to "Cutting Bias Strips" on page 119 to cut the bias strips. Step-by-step instructions for my invisible machine-appliqué method begin on page 121, or you can substitute your own favorite method for cutting the appliqué shapes. The large and small leaf appliqué patterns are provided on page 118.

From the cream print, cut:
2 strips, 1½" × 21"; crosscut into 16 rectangles, 1½" × 2½"
1 strip, 4½" × 21"; crosscut into 1 square, 4½" × 4½". From the remainder of the strip, cut:
    6 rectangles, 1½" × 2½" (combined total of 22 with previously cut rectangles)
    12 squares, 1½" × 1½"

From *each of 3* assorted red print charm squares, cut:
1 square, 2½" × 2½" (combined total of 3)
1 square, 1⅞" × 1⅞" (combined total of 3)
Keep the pieces organized by print into star sets.
    Reserve the remainder of the 3 red charm squares.

From the dark red print, cut:
3 strips, 1½" × 10½"; crosscut into 18 squares, 1½" × 1½"
Reserve the remainder of the dark red print.

From *each of 3* assorted aqua charm squares, cut:
1 strip, 1½" × 5"; crosscut into 3 squares, 1½" × 1½" (combined total of 9)
Keep the pieces organized by print into star base sets.
    Reserve the remainder of the 3 assorted aqua charm squares.

Continued on page 114

Continued from page 113

From the dark teal print, cut:

3 binding strips, 2½" × 21" (for my chubby binding method provided on page 127, reduce the strip width to 2")

1 *bias* strip, 1¼" × 8"

2 *bias* strips, 1¼" × 3"

Reserve the remainder of the dark teal print.

From the 3 unused aqua charm squares, the reserved remainder of the 3 assorted aqua charm squares, and the reserved remainder of the dark teal print, cut a *combined total* of:

4 small leaves

1 large leaf and 1 reversed large leaf

20 squares, 1½" × 1½"

From the medium red check, cut:

2 strips, 1½" × 8½"

2 strips, 1½" × 10½"

From the 3 unused red charm squares, the reserved remainder of the 3 assorted red charm squares, and the reserved remainder of the dark red print, cut a *combined total* of:

20 squares, 1½" × 1½"

PIECING THE STARFLOWER BLOCK

Sew all pieces with right sides together using a ¼" seam allowance. Press the seam allowances as indicated by the arrows or otherwise specified.

1. From freezer paper, use a rotary cutter and an acrylic ruler to cut three squares, 1⅜" × 1⅜"; reserve two of the freezer-paper squares for later use.

2. From one set of red star patchwork pieces, select the red 1⅞" square; reserve the red 2½" square for later use. Apply a small amount of fabric glue stick to the center of the dull, nonwaxy side of a freezer-paper square and affix it shiny side up on the center of the wrong side of the red 1⅞" square. Use a hot, dry iron to press the seam allowance onto the freezer-paper pattern piece. Apply a small bit of glue stick to the bottommost layer of seam allowance at each corner of the square and use a hot iron to heat set and anchor the layers in place so they'll be hidden from the front.

Use a rotary cutter and an acrylic ruler to cut the prepared freezer-paper square in half diagonally to make two red triangles.

3. In addition to the red triangles from step 2 and the reserved red 2½" square, choose one set of three aqua 1½" squares, four cream 1½" × 2½" rectangles, four cream 1½" squares, and six dark red 1½" squares. Use a pencil and an acrylic ruler to draw a diagonal sewing line from corner to corner on the wrong side of each aqua and dark red 1½" square.

4. Fold a cream 1½" × 2½" rectangle in half crosswise and finger-press the center crease. Repeat to prepare two cream rectangles. Using the crease for centering, baste a red triangle onto each of the two prepared cream rectangles, with the bottom raw edges flush. Use your favorite appliqué method to stitch the red triangles in place. Remove the paper pattern pieces. The appliquéd small star-point units should measure 1½" × 2½", including the seam allowances.

Appliqué 2 small star-point units,
1½" × 2½".

5. Layer a prepared dark red 1½" square from step 3 onto an appliquéd small star-point unit as shown. Stitch the pair together along the drawn line. Fold the resulting inner triangle open, aligning the corner with the corner of the small star-point unit. Press. Trim away the layers beneath the top dark red triangle, leaving a ¼" seam allowance. In the same manner, add a mirror-image dark red star-point unit to the remaining end of the unit. Repeat to piece a total of two red triple star-point units measuring 1½" × 2½", including the seam allowances.

Make 2 triple
star-point units,
1½" × 2½".

6. Using two prepared aqua and two prepared dark red 1½" squares, follow step 5 above to piece one

aqua-and-red star-point unit and one aqua-and-red mirror-image star-point unit. Each unit should measure 1½" × 2½", including the seam allowances.

Make 1 of each unit,
1½" × 2½".

7. Use the remaining prepared aqua 1½" square to sew a triangle to one corner of the red 2½" square as previously instructed.

Make 1 center square unit,
2½" × 2½".

8. Referring to "Making Bias-Tube Stems and Vines" on page 123, prepare the dark teal 8"-long center stem and the two 3"-long side stems. Set aside the side stems for later use. Apply a couple of drops of liquid fabric glue to the wrong side of one end of the 8" stem. Affix the stem onto the right side of a cream 1½" square, positioning it diagonally. Heat set the glued end of the stem square from the back, leaving the remainder of the stem unattached.

Glue baste
the end only.

9. Lay out the stem square, the two triple star-point units from step 4, the two aqua-and-red star-point units from step 6, the center square unit from step 7, and three cream 1½" squares in three horizontal rows as shown. Join the pieces in each row. Press. Join the rows. Press. The pieced center star unit should measure 4½" square, including the seam allowances.

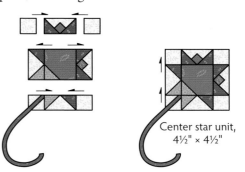

Center star unit,
4½" × 4½".

10. Substituting the prepared 3" teal stems for the 8" stem, repeat steps 2–9 to piece two side star units measuring 4½" square, including the seam allowances.

Make 2 side star units,
4½" × 4½".

11. Pinning the teal stems onto the center square units to keep them free of the areas to be stitched, refer to the quilt pictured on page 116 to lay out the three star units and the cream 4½" square in two horizontal rows. Join the pieces in each row. Press seam allowances

FINISHED QUILT SIZE: 10½" × 14½" ◆ FINISHED BLOCK SIZE: 8" × 8"

Designed, pieced, and machine appliquéd by Kim Diehl. Machine quilted by Rebecca Silbaugh.

Tussie-Mussie

open. Join the rows. Press the seam allowances open. The pieced Starflower block should now measure 8½" square, including the seam allowances.

12. Apply dots of liquid fabric glue to the wrong side of the 8" teal stem at about ½" intervals; affix it diagonally to the block unit. In the same manner, glue baste and position the 3" side stems, trimming away any excess length and tucking the raw ends under the center stem. Lay out and baste four small leaves, one large leaf, and one mirror-image large leaf as shown. Use your favorite method to appliqué the stems and leaves in place.

Starflower block,
8½" × 8½"

ADDING THE BORDERS

1. Referring to the adding the borders illustration at right, join a red check 1½" × 8½" strip to the right and left sides of the Starflower block. Press. Join a red check 1½" × 10½" strip to each remaining side of the block. Press. The quilt top should measure 10½" square, including the seam allowances.

2. Choosing the prints randomly, lay out and join 10 assorted aqua 1½" squares end to end. Press. Repeat to piece two aqua checkerboard units measuring 1½" × 10½", including the seam allowances. Join these pieced units to the top and bottom edges of the quilt top. Press.

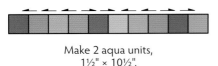

Make 2 aqua units,
1½" × 10½".

3. Draw a diagonal sewing line from corner to corner on the wrong side of each assorted red 1½" square as previously instructed. Using the prepared red 1½" squares and the remaining 10 cream 1½" × 2½" rectangles, stitch 10 flying-geese units measuring 1½" × 2½", as previously instructed.

Make 10 units,
1½" × 2½".

4. Lay out and join five flying-geese units end to end. Press. Repeat to piece two flying-geese border strips measuring 1½" × 10½", including the seam allowances.

Make 2 flying-geese border strips,
1½" × 10½".

5. Join the flying-geese strips to the top and bottom edges of the quilt top. Press.

Adding borders

COMPLETING THE QUILT

Layer and baste the quilt top, batting, and backing. Quilt the layers. The featured quilt was machine quilted in the ditch (along the seam lines) around the outer portions of the star units, with diagonal lines radiating out from the center of the aqua bases to fill the red star centers, and the aqua bases were stitched with curved lines to anchor the center areas. The stems and appliqués were outlined to emphasize their shapes, and the cream background areas of the Starflower block were quilted with repeating curved lines to create an "oil slick" pattern. The inner border was stitched with repeating straight lines. The checkerboard border was stitched with double diagonal lines to create a zigzag herringbone pattern, and the cream portions of the outer flying-geese border were stitched with repeating straight lines radiating out vertically from the quilt center. Last, the flying-geese triangles were stitched in the ditch. Join the dark teal binding strips to make one length and use it to bind the quilt.

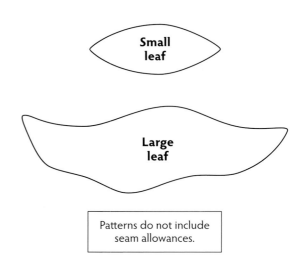

Small leaf

Large leaf

Patterns do not include seam allowances.

Kim's Quiltmaking Basics

The section that follows provides tons of "how-to" information to guide you through the quiltmaking steps in a simple and approachable way. For even more details to round out and build your quiltmaking skills, please visit ShopMartingale.com/HowtoQuilt, where you can download free illustrated guidelines.

ROTARY CUTTING

Unless otherwise instructed, all pieces should be cut across the width of the fabric, from selvage to selvage. To streamline this step, I routinely fold my pressed fabric in half with the selvage edges together, and then align them with a marked line on the cutting mat. For the smaller-scale patchwork featured in this book, I often fold the fabric in half once more to achieve four layered pieces with each cut.

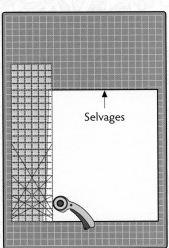

Selvages

CUTTING BIAS STRIPS

1. After pressing the fabric to remove any wrinkles, lay it in a single layer on a large cutting mat. Fold one corner of the cloth back to form a two-layered triangle, aligning the straight edges of the fabric.

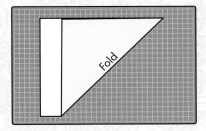

2. Rotate the layered piece of cloth to align the long diagonal fold with a marked line on the cutting mat (this will prevent a dogleg curve in the strips after they've been cut and unfolded).

3. Use a rotary cutter and an acrylic ruler to cut through the folded edge of cloth a few inches in from one pointed end. Work outward from this straight edge to cut strips in the width specified in the project directions.

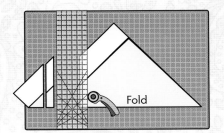

4. Square off the strip ends and trim them to the needed stem length, or join multiple squared-off lengths to form the specified length for vines or binding strips.

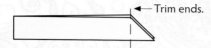

←— Trim ends.

Pinning

I recommend pinning your patchwork at regular intervals, including all sewn seams. I routinely pin the bottom edge of each patchwork unit (where fishtailing can occur), as this enables me to lay my fingertip over the pinhead to guide the unit under the presser foot in a straight line.

Machine Piecing

Unless otherwise instructed, always join your fabrics with right sides together using a ¼" seam allowance. I prefer to shorten my sewing machine's stitch length from 2.2 to 1.8 for all patchwork projects to produce secure, less visible seams from edge to edge.

For projects with many patchwork units to be joined, chain piecing is an ideal way to simultaneously increase your speed *and* save thread. Simply feed the pieces through the sewing machine one after the other without snipping the threads in between; once the stitching is complete, cut the threads between units to separate them.

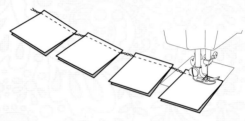

Pressing Seams

1. Place the pieced patchwork unit on your ironing surface with the fabric you wish to press toward on top. Bring the iron down onto the sewn seam to warm the fabric. While the fabric is still warm, fold the top layer of cloth back and run your fingernail along the line of stitching to open the layers all the way to the seam line. Press the opened layers with a hot, dry iron. The seam allowances will now lie under the fabric that was originally positioned on top.

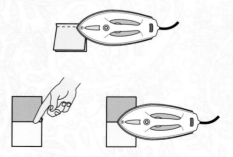

2. Once the block or patchwork unit is complete, lay it wrong side up on the ironing surface, apply a light mist of Best Press (or water), and use a hot iron to set the seams firmly in place. Pressing from the back of your work will help ensure that the seams are resting flat and in the intended direction.

STITCH-AND-FOLD TRIANGLE UNITS

1. After cutting the pieces specified in the project instructions, use a pencil and an acrylic ruler to draw a diagonal sewing line from corner to corner on the wrong side of the square that will be used to stitch the triangle. Layer and stitch the patchwork, sewing the pair together along the drawn line.

2. Fold the resulting inner triangle open, aligning the corner with the corner of the square or rectangle beneath it to keep it square. Press. Trim away the layers beneath the top triangle, leaving ¼" seam allowances.

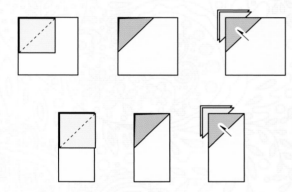

Traditionally, the excess layers beneath the top triangle are trimmed *before* the unit is pressed, but I've found that changing the order of the steps helps produce more accurate results and often eliminates the need to square up the finished unit.

INVISIBLE MACHINE APPLIQUÉ

In addition to standard quiltmaking supplies, you need the following items for my invisible machine-appliqué method:

- Sewing machine with an open-toe presser foot, featuring adjustable tension and the ability to produce a tiny zigzag stitch
- .004 monofilament thread in smoke and clear colors
- Awl or stiletto with a *sharp* point
- Bias bars in various widths
- Embroidery scissors with a fine, sharp point
- Freezer paper

- Lightweight iron or travel-size iron with a pointed pressing tip
- Fabric glue in both liquid *and* stick form, water-soluble (not permanent) and acid-free
- Pressing board with a *firm* surface
- Size 75/11 machine quilting or 60/8 universal sewing-machine needles
- Tweezers with rounded tips

Preparing Pattern-Tracing Templates

A tracing *template* is simply a tool that enables you to easily and consistently duplicate shapes when making multiple pattern pieces, eliminating the need to trace over the top of a pattern sheet numerous times. Remember, any time a pattern template is used, only one will be needed.

1. To prepare a tracing template, cut a single piece of freezer paper about twice as large as your shape. Use a pencil to trace the pattern onto the dull, nonwaxy side of the paper.

2. Fold the freezer paper in half, waxy sides together, and use a hot, dry iron to fuse the layers. From this fused piece, cut out the shape on the drawn lines to produce a sturdy template that can easily be traced around.

Preparing Freezer-Paper Pattern Pieces

Pattern *pieces* are the individual freezer-paper shapes used to prepare and stitch the appliqués from cloth. Always cut paper pattern pieces on the drawn lines, as the seam allowances will be added later when the appliqués are cut from fabric.

Use the prepared tracing template (or pattern sheet, if only a handful of pieces are needed) to trace the specified number of shapes onto the dull, nonwaxy side of a piece of freezer paper. Cut out the shapes on the drawn lines.

To easily make multiple pattern pieces, stack up to five additional layers of freezer paper underneath the top traced piece, all with the dull, nonwaxy paper sides up. Anchor the center of the shape with a pin to prevent shifting *or* use staples at regular intervals in the background around the shape. Cut out the pattern pieces on the drawn lines and discard the background areas.

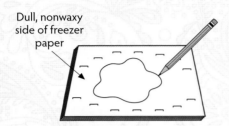

Dull, nonwaxy side of freezer paper

To prepare mirror-image pattern pieces, trace the pattern onto the dull, nonwaxy paper end of a strip of freezer paper, and then fold it accordion-style in widths to fit your shape. Anchor the layers and cut out the pieces as previously instructed. When the layers are separated, every other piece will be a mirror image.

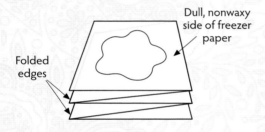

Dull, nonwaxy side of freezer paper

Folded edges

Preparing the Appliqués

1. Apply a small amount of fabric glue stick to the center of the dull, nonwaxy side of a freezer-paper pattern piece; affix the pattern piece to the *wrong* side of the fabric, *shiny side up*. Repeat with the remaining pattern pieces, leaving approximately ½" between each shape on the fabric for seam allowances.

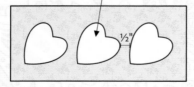

Wrong side of fabric, freezer paper waxy side up

½"

2. Using embroidery scissors, cut out each shape, adding an approximate ¼" seam allowance around the paper. Keep in mind that cutting the seam allowance in too scant a width will make it difficult to work with, while cutting too thick a width will add bulk. As you practice the preparation steps and become comfortable

with this technique, you'll find the width that works perfectly for you.

3. To make it easier to finish the appliqué edges, clip the seam allowance at any pronounced *inner* point or curve, stopping a couple threads away from the paper pattern piece. It isn't necessary to clip the seam allowances along any outer curves or points, only the inner portions.

Clip inner points, almost to paper edge.

Pressing Appliqués

Keep in mind as you work through the steps that follow that you'll want to work along the edge of the appliqué that's farthest away from you, rotating the appliqué toward the point of your iron as you work in one direction from start to finish. Always begin pressing along a straight edge or at a gentle curve, *never* at a point or a corner, because this approach will direct the seam allowance toward your "smart" hand (which is the hand that will hold the awl or stiletto) for later steps.

1. Use the pad of your finger to smooth the fabric seam allowance over onto the waxy side of the paper pattern piece, following with the point of a hot, dry iron to firmly press the cloth in place. (Please note that no glue is needed for this step, because there's enough "stick" on the waxy surface to hold the fabric in place on the paper pattern piece.) To avoid puckered appliqué edges, always draw the seam allowance slightly back toward the last section pressed, letting the point of the iron rest on each newly pressed area as you draw the next bit of cloth onto the pattern piece.

Direct seam allowance toward center of shape.

2. For sharp outer points, press the seam allowance so the folded edge extends beyond the paper pattern point. Fold over the seam allowance of the remaining side of the point and continue to complete the pressing. Apply a small amount of glue stick to the bottom of the folded flap of seam allowance at the point. Use the point of an awl or stiletto to drag the fabric in and away from the appliqué edge (not *down* from the point, as this will blunt it), and press with the point of the iron to fuse the layers in place. To hide the seam allowance at a narrow point, roll the seam allowance slightly under as you draw it in from the edge with the awl.

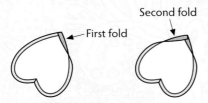

First fold

Second fold

To help achieve beautiful, sharp appliqué points, ensure that your pressed seam allowance hugs the paper edge on both sides of any given point as shown.

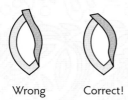

Wrong   Correct!

3. To prepare an inner point, stop pressing the seam allowance just shy of the center clipped section. Reaching under the appliqué at the clip, use the pad of your finger or the point of an awl to draw the clipped section of fabric snugly onto the paper, following immediately with the iron to fuse the cloth in place.

Making Bias-Tube Stems and Vines

To achieve finished stems and vines that can be curved flawlessly and don't require the seam allowances to be turned under, I use bias tubes. After cutting the strips specified in the project instructions (and referring to "Cutting Bias Strips" on page 119), prepare them as follows.

1. With *wrong* sides together (you'll want to be looking at the pretty, finished side of the print as you work through this step), fold the strip in half lengthwise. Use a slightly scant ¼" seam allowance to stitch along the long raw edges to form a tube. For narrow stems, you'll likely need to trim the seam allowance to approximately ⅛" so that it will be hidden from the front of the finished stem.

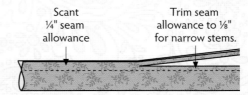

Scant ¼" seam allowance

Trim seam allowance to ⅛" for narrow stems.

2. Because of possible seam allowance differences, the *best* bias-bar width for each project can vary from the size specified. Ultimately, choose a bar that will fit comfortably into the sewn tube, positioning the seam allowance so it's resting flat to one side (not open), and centered from side to side. Press.

Bias bar

3. After removing the bias bar, place small dots of liquid fabric glue at approximately ½" intervals underneath the pressed seam allowance. Use a hot iron to heat set the glue and fuse the seam-allowance layers in place.

Basting Appliqués

Keep in mind as you lay out your design and baste the appliqués that there should be approximately ½" between the outermost appliqués and the raw edge of the background to preserve an intact margin of space around each piece.

1. Lay out the prepared appliqués on the background to establish the design, with any raw edges overlapped approximately ¼".

2. Remove all but the bottommost appliqués, and then baste them in place. My preferred method for this is glue basting because there are no pins to stitch around, the appliqués won't shift, and the background cloth won't shrink during the stitching process.

To glue baste, fold over one half of a positioned shape to expose the back; place small dots of liquid fabric glue along the fabric seam allowance (avoiding the paper pattern piece) at approximately ½" intervals. Unfold and reposition the glue-basted portion of the appliqué, repeat with the remaining half of the shape, and use a hot, dry iron from the back of the unit to heat set the glue and anchor the shape in place.

Preparing Your Sewing Machine

As you prepare your sewing machine, be sure to match the monofilament thread to your appliqué, choosing the smoke color for medium and dark prints and clear for bright colors and pastels.

1. Insert a size 75/11 machine-quilting needle (or a smaller 60/8 universal needle) in your sewing machine and thread it with monofilament.

2. Wind the bobbin with all-purpose neutral-colored thread. I suggest avoiding prewound bobbins because they can sometimes make it difficult to achieve perfectly balanced tension.

Note: If your machine's bobbin case features a "finger" with a special eye for use with embroidery techniques, feed your thread through this opening to help further regulate the tension.

3. Set your sewing machine to the zigzag stitch, adjust the width and length to achieve a tiny stitch as shown, and reduce the tension setting. For many sewing machines, a setting of 1 for the width, length, and tension produces the perfect stitch.

∿∿∿∿∿∿∿∿∿∿∿∿

Approximate stitch size

Stitching the Appliqués

The following steps will guide you through the stitching process. With a little practice, it's fun and easy!

1. Slide the basted appliqué under the presser foot from front to back to direct the threads behind the machine, positioning it to the left of the needle. Beginning at a straight or gently curved edge, anchor the monofilament tail with your finger as your machine takes two or three stitches. Release the thread and continue zigzag stitching around the shape, with the inner stitches landing just inside the appliqué and the outer stitches piercing the background immediately next to the appliqué. After a short distance, clip the monofilament thread tail.

2. Continue stitching the appliqué at a slow to moderate speed, stopping and pivoting as often as needed to keep the edge of your shape feeding straight toward the needle.

- If dots of bobbin thread appear along the top surface edge of your appliqué as you stitch, further reduce the tension setting until they disappear.

- If the monofilament thread underneath your appliqué is visible from the back, or the stitches appear loose or loopy, gradually increase the tension setting as you stitch until they're secure.

3. For a secure inner appliqué point, stitch to the position where the inner stitch rests exactly inside the point of the shape and then stop. Pivot the piece and continue stitching.

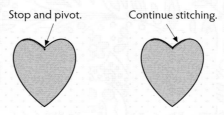

Stop and pivot.   Continue stitching.

4. To secure an outer appliqué point, stitch to the position where the outer stitch lands exactly next to the appliqué point in the background and then stop. Pivot the piece and continue stitching.

Stop and pivot.

Continue stitching.

5. As you complete the stitching, overlap the starting point by approximately ¼" and end with a locking stitch. For machines without a locking stitch, extend your overlapped area to be approximately ½" long and your appliqué will remain secure.

String Appliqué

When two or more appliqués are positioned close together on the same layer, I recommend stitching your first appliqué as instructed in "Stitching the Appliqués" on page 124, but instead of clipping the threads when you finish, lift the presser foot and slide the background to the next appliqué without lifting it from the sewing-machine surface. Lower the presser foot and resume stitching the next appliqué, remembering to end with a locking stitch or overlap your starting position by ¼" to ½". After the cluster of appliqués has been stitched, carefully clip the threads between each one.

Removing Paper Pattern Pieces

On the wrong side of the stitched appliqué, use embroidery scissors to carefully pinch and cut through the background fabric approximately ¼" inside the appliqué seam. Trim away the background, leaving a generous ¼" seam allowance. Grasp the appliqué edge between the thumb and finger of one hand and grab the seam allowances immediately opposite with the other hand. Give a gentle but firm tug to free the paper edge. Next, use your fingertip to loosen the glue anchoring the pattern piece to the fabric; peel away the paper. Any paper scraps that remain in the appliqué corners can be grabbed and pulled out with a pair of tweezers.

FINISHING TECHNIQUES

The guidelines that follow provide a variety of options for you to finish and personalize the look of your quilt.

Batting

For quilt tops using prewashed fabrics, I suggest using polyester batting or a cotton/polyester blend to ensure minimal shrinkage if your quilt is laundered. For quilt tops stitched from fabrics that weren't prewashed, I recommend choosing cotton batting, particularly if you love the slightly puckered look of vintage quilts.

Backing

I cut and piece my quilt backings to be approximately 3" larger than my quilt on each side. To prevent shadowing, it's generally best to use fabrics in colors similar to those in your quilt top.

Basting

For the smaller-sized projects featured in this book, I love the convenience of sandwiching the layers with basting spray, following the manufacturer's instructions. Additional basting methods can be found at ShopMartingale.com/HowtoQuilt.

Marking Quilting Designs

Masking tape or blue painter's tape in various widths makes an ideal guide for stitching straight lines. If you choose this method, keep in mind that all pieces of tape should be removed from the quilt top at the end of each day to prevent a sticky residue from forming on the cloth. More elaborate designs can be marked onto the top using a fine-tipped water-soluble marker before the layers are basted together.

Big-Stitch Hand Quilting

The big-stitch style of hand quilting is one of my favorite methods, because it's a quick and easy way to include hand stitching in my projects without a huge investment of time. For this style of quilting, I use a size 5 embroidery needle and #12 perle cotton to sew a running stitch (with each stitch approximately ⅛" to a scant ¼" long) through the quilt layers, ending my stitches as I would for traditional hand quilting.

Portable Sewing Station

If you're anything like me and you're tired of chasing spools of sewing thread and perle cotton across tabletops and underneath your sofas, here's a great solution. Grab a short, wide-mouth canning jar, discard the metal cap that fits inside the lid, and then drop in your thread. Place a frog insert onto the jar rim, weaving your thread tails up through the metal grid, and replace the lid. Frog inserts are typically used for flower arrangements and can be found in craft stores and through online retailers; they easily transform everyday jars into the best portable sewing stations. These also make fantastic gifts for quilting friends, especially when filled with your favorite thread, a cute little pair of scissors, and a handful of chocolate kisses!

Machine Quilting

For in-depth machine-quilting instructions, please refer to *25 Days to Better Machine Quilting* by Lori Kennedy (Martingale, 2020).

You'll see an edge-to-edge swirling pattern (think cinnamon rolls!) on many of my quilts when I want to add texture without introducing another design element. This pattern is shown below and is easy to stitch!

Start here.

Chubby Binding

Traditionally, a 2½"-wide French-fold binding is used to finish most quilts; step-by-step instructions can be found at ShopMartingale.com/HowtoQuilt. For my quilts, I prefer a more unconventional "chubby binding" method to produce a traditional look from the front of the quilt, with a wide strip of binding on the back.

To stitch chubby binding, you'll need 2"-wide strips and a bias-tape maker designed to produce 1"-wide double-fold tape.

1. Join the 2"-wide strips end to end without pressing the seam allowances. Next, slide the pieced strip through the bias-tape maker, pressing the folds with a hot, dry iron as they emerge, and the seams will automatically be directed to one side as the strip is pressed.

2. Open the fold of the strip along the top edge only. Turn the beginning raw edge under ½" and finger-press the fold. Starting along one side of the quilt top (not at a corner), align the unfolded raw edge of the binding with the raw edge of the quilt. Use a ¼" seam allowance to stitch the binding along the raw edges. Stop sewing ¼" from the first corner and backstitch. Clip the thread and remove the quilt from under the presser foot.

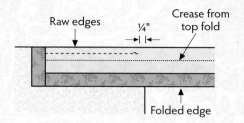

Raw edges
¼"
Crease from top fold
Folded edge

3. Make a fold in the binding, then bring it up and back down onto itself to square the corner. Rotate the quilt 90° and reposition it under the presser foot. Resume sewing at the top edge of the quilt, continuing around the perimeter in this manner.

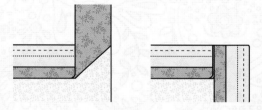

4. When you approach your starting point, cut the end to extend 1" beyond the folded edge and complete the stitching.

5. Bring the wide folded edge of the binding to the back and hand stitch it to the back of the quilt, enclosing the raw edges. Use a blind stitch and matching thread to hand sew the binding to the back. At each corner, fold the binding to form a miter and hand stitch it in place.

About the Author

After falling in love with a sampler quilt pattern in the late 1990s, Kim impulsively purchased it, taught herself the steps needed to make it, and then realized she was smitten with quiltmaking. As her newfound passion blossomed into a full-time career, Kim began publishing her original designs, traveled nationally to teach her approachable quiltmaking methods, and ultimately began designing fabrics . . . a dream come true for a girl who once wondered if she had what it took to make a single quilt!

Using modern time-saving techniques enables Kim to be prolific in her quiltmaking, and something new is always in the works. Her very favorite quilts feature scrappy color schemes sewn from a mix of richly hued prints, and they often blend traditionally inspired patchwork with appliqué designs.

In addition to authoring numerous books, including her Simple series with Martingale, Kim continues to design quilting fabric collections and Simple Whatnots Club projects in her signature scrap-basket style for Henry Glass & Co.

Since retiring from an extensive travel and teaching schedule in 2015, Kim now spends her days at home doing what she loves most—designing quilts and fabrics, baking, stitching, gardening, and being a nana to her two young granddaughters as she teaches them to love all things creative.